/E2

Maths
The Basic Skills

Measure,
Shape and
Space

June Haighton • Veronica Thomas

Published in 2004 by:
Nelson Thornes Ltd
Delta Place
27 Bath Road
CHELTENHAM
GL53 7TH
United Kingdom

05 06 07 08/10 9 8 7 6 5 4 3

A catalogue record for this book is available from the British Library

ISBN 0 7487 7863 2

Illustrations by Mathematical Composition Setters Ltd, Salisbury, Wiltshire and Oxford Designers and Illustrators
Page make-up by Mathematical Composition Setters Ltd, Salisbury, Wiltshire

Printed and bound in Croatia by Zrinski

Contents

Activities

Instructions

Time

Length

(N.B. Students should only measure the front edge of the cube and pyramid.)

Weight

Capacity

Resources

About the Measures, Shape and Space Worksheet Pack

This Worksheet Pack contains Activities, Worksheets and other Resources for students who are working on topics from the Measures, Shape and Space section of the Adult Numeracy Core Curriculum at Entry levels 1 and 2 (E1 and E2).

Entry level 3 (E3), Level 1 (L1) and Level 2 (L2) are covered in the textbook **Maths: The Basic Skills. Curriculum Edition.**

Activities

This section includes games and other activities. The instructions for these are grouped together at the start of the section with the corresponding card sheets following behind. In most cases you will need to photocopy a sheet onto card then laminate and cut out the pieces you need for the game or activity.

Worksheets

These are arranged in order of topics as follows:
- Money
- Time
- Length
- Weight
- Capacity
- Temperature
- Scales
- Shape

Where a topic covers more than one level the worksheets are arranged in order of curriculum reference, starting with E1 before progressing to E2

The curriculum element covered by a worksheet is indicated alongside the title of the worksheet and also on the sheet itself.

Resource sheets

This section contains additional resources to help with your teaching.

Answers

Answers to the Worksheets can be found online at www.nelsonthornes.com/mathsthebasicskills

How to use this Worksheet Pack

Use the contents list to find out which Activities or Worksheets will help you to teach a particular topic or curriculum reference. The tabs on the side of the pages will help you to locate the sheet you need.

Instructions

N.B. Sheets of cards need to be photocopied onto card, laminated and cut out before use. Until they are confident in the group, students may be unwilling to make an individual response and it is important that they do not feel they have failed. For these reasons it is recommended that in mental maths games you ask all students to respond at the same time.

Money

Money dominoes

MSS1/E1.1

NEEDED
Money domino cards
Selection of 5p, 2p, and 1p coins

WHAT TO DO   *(2 players)*

Tutor places a selection of coins on the table. Each player has 7 cards. Spare cards are put in a pile face down. The first player chooses one of their cards and puts it face up on the table, then selects coins to the value shown and puts them on top of the card. Players then take turns to place a card on the table matching the written version with the figures and putting appropriate coins on top. Whenever the wrong money is used, the card is taken back and the player loses a turn. If a player has no matching card, they pick one up off the pile. The winner is the first player to have played all their cards.

Money dominoes – coins and notes

MSS1/E1.1

NEEDED
Money dominoes – coin and note cards/ actual coins and notes if possible

WHAT TO DO

Individually or in pairs, form a circle matching each domino's value to picture. If actual coins and notes are available, match these as well.

Which coins would you give?

MSS1/E2.1

NEEDED
Number cards
Selection of coins

WHAT TO DO

Tutor places 2 cards together face up on the table (e.g. 2 and a 3 so that they show 23). Students pick the coins needed for 23p. These are kept hidden until all students are ready. Coins are shown by all students at the same time.

Make it games

These games can be played either with the note cards or the coin cards, with the appropriate Make It Cards. If possible, matching the cards with actual coins or notes would be beneficial. Other amounts can be given.

Game 1

MSS1/E1.1 or MSS1/E2.1

NEEDED
note or coin cards (select according to level)

WHAT TO DO

Each student has one note card, placed face up in front of them. The tutor says an amount e.g. £7 (up to £9 for E1.1). The students work out which cards/students need to go together to make this amount.

Game 2

MSS1/E2.1

NEEDED
note or coin cards and appropriate To Make cards

WHAT TO DO

Each student has 2 note or coin cards placed face up in front of them. Remaining cards are put in a pile. In turn, students pick up a To Make card. Either the student makes the amount from their own coin/note cards, or they pick an extra note/coin card. When all coin/note cards have been used, students can take a card from another student to add to their own to make the amount shown on the To Make card. If a student is unable to make the amount, they miss a go. The winner is the first student to use all their note/coin cards.

Game 3 – for smaller groups

MSS1/E2.1

NEEDED
note or coin cards/ To Make cards

WHAT TO DO

The note or coin cards are divided between the group. The To Make cards are placed face down in a pile. In turn students pick a To Make card and try to make it with their own cards. The winner is the student who has completed the most To Make cards.

Game 4 – small group/pair or individual

MSS1/E2.1

NEEDED
note or coin cards/ To Make cards

WHAT TO DO

Students match the coins/notes with the To Make cards in such a way that all the To Make cards are completed.

How many 10p coins?

MSS1/E2.1

NEEDED
Multiples of 10p cards
Pen and wipe sheet (A4 plain sheet of paper in plastic wallet) for each student

WHAT TO DO

Tutor holds a card up facing the students. Students write on their sheet the number of 10p coins needed to make this amount. When all students are ready they show their answers at the same time.

Change from £1 – using multiples of 10p

MSS1/E2.2

NEEDED
Multiples of 10p cards
Pen and wipe sheet (A4 plain sheet of paper in plastic wallet) for each student

WHAT TO DO

Tutor explains that the students are each starting with £1. Tutor holds a card up facing the students – this represents the amount to be taken away. Students write down the change. All show responses at the same time.

Change from £1 – using all numbers

MSS1/E2.2

NEEDED
Number cards
Pen and wipe sheet (A4 plain sheet of paper in plastic wallet) for each student

WHAT TO DO

Tutor explains that they are each starting with £1. Tutor puts 2 cards face up together (e.g. 29) – this represents the amount to be taken away. Students write down the change. All show responses at the same time.

Change from £20 – using whole £s

MSS1/E2.2

NEEDED
£ cards up to £20 (may need 2 sets depending on group size)

WHAT TO DO

£ cards are shuffled and placed face down on the table. The first player turns a card over then subtracts the amount from £20. If the player gets the correct answer, they keep the cards. Play goes around the group until all cards are used. For a more difficult game the player turns over 2 cards and finds the change from £20 (or subtracts the lower amount from the higher amount.) For mixed ability, tutors may want to provide different card sets to individual students to enable them to work with certain numbers.

Time

Match the month dominoes

MSS1/E2.3

NEEDED
Match the month dominoes

WHAT TO DO *(2 or 3 players)*

Share dominoes between players. Put spare dominoes in a pile face down. The first player chooses a domino and puts it face up on the table. Players then take turns to place a domino matching the months. Whenever the months are wrongly matched the domino is taken back and the player loses a turn. If a player has no matching domino, they pick one up off the pile. The winner is the first player to have played all their dominoes.

Match the times

MSS1/E2.4

NEEDED
Time cards (set of matching analogue and digital clocks)

WHAT TO DO *(individually or as a group)*

Choose the cards for the level of the students – hours/$\frac{1}{2}$ hours/$\frac{1}{4}$ hours. Match the clock faces.

Add on/take off

MSS1/E2.4

NEEDED
Time cards (set of analogue and digital clocks) Period of time cards

WHAT TO DO *(individually or as a group)*

In a group, answers can be spoken or written down on a wipe board and all shown at the same time. If the group covers different levels, the tutor can hold the cards, selecting for each student as appropriate.

Choose from:

A Time in hours   add on/take off   1 hour(s)

B Time in hours and halves   2 half

C Time in hours and quarters   3 quarter

                                         4 three quarters

                                         5 hour(s) + half or + quarter(s)

A time card is shown, e.g. `08:00` AM PM

State whether adding on, or taking off, e.g. adding

A period of time card is shown, e.g. | 2 hours |

The student adds the 2 hours on to the time card, e.g. answer 10 o'clock.

Length

All of these activities work best with real objects.

Bigger/smaller A

MSS1/E1.3

NEEDED
Various objects/ Animal cards

WHAT TO DO *(small groups led by tutor/helper)*

Objects/cards are shared between the students. The leader states 'Big', 'Small', 'Bigger than a ...' or 'Smaller than a ...'. Players place appropriate objects/cards in front of them. These can be shown altogether to make it easier for new/hesitant students. (Can be used to develop discussion using other words that describe size – huge, tiny, little, etc.)

Bigger/smaller B

MSS1/E1.3

NEEDED

Various objects/**Animal cards**

Size word cards – bigger, smaller

WHAT TO DO *(for a group of students, not led by the tutor)*

Place an object (or picture card) on the table and share the remaining objects (cards) between players. Players can look at their own objects (cards), but they must be hidden from other players (use a bag for each player to keep objects in). Tutor states 'Bigger' or 'Smaller' to start the game. If 'Bigger', the first player has to choose a bigger object from their bag. If choosing a card, the object represented should be bigger. This is placed beside the first object (card) on the table. This player now decides 'Bigger' or 'Smaller' (showing the appropriate word card). The second player places an appropriate object on the table and decides 'Bigger' or 'Smaller' and so on. If an object is incorrect, the player takes back the object. If a player is unable to go, they miss a turn. N.B. Players must be able to place an object themselves when they decide on 'Bigger' or 'Smaller'. The winner is the first person to use all their objects (cards).

Ordering

MSS1/E1.3

NEEDED

Various objects/ **Animal cards**

Size word cards – largest, smallest, biggest

WHAT TO DO *(individually or in pairs or small groups)*

A number of objects/cards are selected. Students put the objects/cards in order of size, then place the word cards appropriately.

Drawing – bigger, larger, smaller

MSS1/E1.3

NEEDED

Shape cards

Size word cards – bigger, larger, smaller

WHAT TO DO *(individually or in small groups/pairs)*

Shape cards are distributed. Students put their shapes (e.g. 3 circles) in order of size. Each student then picks a word card, draws an appropriate shape (i.e. bigger, larger or smaller than all the others) and puts it in the correct place in line with the others.

Longer/shorter/wider/taller

MSS1/E1.4

NEEDED

Shape cards
Length word cards – longer, shorter, wider, taller, narrower

WHAT TO DO *(individually or in small groups or pairs)*

Play in the same way as **Bigger/smaller** above. When tutor-led, this can involve discussion about what is considered long, tall, short, wide, narrow, etc. The ideas from E1.3 and E1.4 can also be linked, e.g.   It is bigger – it is longer.

It is smaller – it is not as wide.

Ordering

MSS1/E1.4

NEEDED

Various objects/ **Size cards**

Length word cards – longest, tallest, widest, thinnest

WHAT TO DO *(individually or in small groups/pairs)*

As in E1.3, but with different words.

Drawing

NEEDED
Shape cards – rectangles/Size cards
Length word cards – longer, narrower, shorter, thinner

WHAT TO DO

Distribute shape cards. These are put in order of size. Each student then picks a word card, draws an appropriate shape and puts it in the correct place with the other cards. This can also be done with circles and squares – leading to discussions on a wider circle/square is also taller, etc.

Weight

It is important for students to compare real objects and estimate/guess which is heavier or lighter before applying the concept with picture cards. At this stage, a simple balance scale is useful to check answers when students compare the weight of 2 objects held in their hands.

The following games can be played with real objects as well as with the picture cards supplied for MSS1/E1.5 (cards for E1.3 games can also be used).

Heavier/lighter

NEEDED
Objects/**Weight cards**
Weight word cards – heavier, lighter

WHAT TO DO

Play as in 'Bigger/smaller' MSS1/E1.3, but using the words 'heavier/lighter'. If using real objects, encourage students to hold the object to get an idea of its weight. With actual objects use a balance scale to confirm answers.

Ordering

NEEDED
Objects/**Weight cards**
Weight word cards – heaviest, lightest

WHAT TO DO

Put 3, 4 or 5 items in order of their weights, then place the 'heaviest/lightest' cards appropriately. (Always use the balance scale to check the answers with actual objects.)

Find an object

NEEDED
Weight cards
Weight word cards – heavier, lighter

WHAT TO DO

Place all the picture cards face down on the table. Have the 'heavier/lighter' cards in a pile, the top one showing, e.g. 'heavier'. The first player turns one picture card over. The second player looks at the word card then turns over another picture card. If this picture card represents an object heavier than the first picture card shown, the player takes both of the picture cards. The 'heavier' card is put on the bottom of the pile. If the object represented is lighter, both of the picture cards are turned over. The second player turns over the first picture card for the next player.

Weight order

NEEDED
A selection of food items: tins, packets, cartons, etc.
Balance/weighing scales

WHAT TO DO   *(individually or as a group)*

Without looking at the labels the students attempt to list the items in order of weight. Then students look at the labels, make a second list of the items in weight order and compare the two lists. (Also weigh each item to check if the given weight on the packets is correct.)

Activities

Capacity

How much?

NEEDED

Similar shaped containers containing different quantities of liquid e.g. glasses/ mugs (if possible one for each student in a group)

WHAT TO DO   (small group or individually)

Discuss

a Who has the **most**/**least**?

b Has anyone got a **full** glass?

c Has anyone got an **empty** glass?

d Who has **more than** the others?

e Who has **less than** the others?

f Who needs **more** to make it fair?

If students are unsure, check the volume, e.g. by counting the number of egg cups the liquid from each glass fills.

Most or least A

NEEDED

3 or 4 similar shaped glasses or mugs containing different amounts of liquid.

Capacity cards – holds most, holds least

WHAT TO DO

Put the containers in order, with the words 'most/least' placed appropriately.

Most or least B

NEEDED

As in A, but using the pictures from **Capacity cards** instead

WHAT TO DO

When students are confident judging 'most/least' with similar shaped glasses, the activities can be done with different shapes.

Most or least C

NEEDED

2 glasses – one tall and thin, the other short and wide

2 similar shaped glasses

WHAT TO DO

Pour drink to the same level in the tall/thin glass and the short/wide glass. Discuss which holds more and why. Prove the difference by pouring the drink into the other 2 similar shaped glasses.

Most or least D

NEEDED

Variety of glasses including some with thick/thin glass or thick glass bottoms

WHAT TO DO

Pour drink to the same level in the glasses. Discuss which holds the most and why. Prove the difference by pouring the drink into similar shaped glasses. Extend the choice to include other containers, e.g. various shaped pots, pans and dishes.

Estimate/measure capacity

MSS1/E2.7

NEEDED
A selection of containers – common household ones are best, measuring jugs, etc.

WHAT TO DO   *(individually or as a group)*

Without looking at the capacity on the labels, the students attempt to list the containers in order of capacity. Then students use the labels to list the containers in order of capacity and compare the lists. (Also measure the capacity of each container to check that the given capacity is correct.)

Shape

Wallpaper shapes

MSS2/E1.1/E2.1

NEEDED
Wallpaper samples

WHAT TO DO

1 Sort the samples according to shape:
   ● those with rectangular, square, circular, triangular patterns
   ● patterns with two or more shapes.
2 Cut out different sized circles, rectangles, squares and triangles. Put into size order.
3 Make collages with different shapes.

Properties of shape

MSS2/E2.2

NEEDED
Various boxes/ packets

WHAT TO DO

Sort according to 3-D shape, shape of faces, number of edges, number of corners.

Deliver the message – positional vocabulary

MSS2/E2.3

NEEDED
Prior to the session, ask some other tutors to help by accepting messages. Simple map of the building, simple messages requiring yes/no answers

WHAT TO DO

1 Follow short simple verbal directions involving left, right, etc. to deliver a message.
2 Follow a simple plan of the building to deliver a message.

Follow the route

MSS2/E2.3

NEEDED
Simple local map of the area showing the centre and some of the local amenities, e.g. shops, bus stops, school, church. Written directions (left, right, etc.)

WHAT TO DO

Students follow directions to show the route on the map from the centre:
i   to home
ii   to any local amenity
iii between different amenities in the area.

I spy

MSS2/E2.3

WHAT TO DO   *(small group with everyone facing the same direction)*

'I spy something ...' on our right/left/above us, etc.

Find the object

NEEDED
A collection of 3-D shapes on a table, labelled 1, 2, 3 etc.

WHAT TO DO   *(small group with everyone facing in the same direction)*

One person chooses an object. The others ask questions to find the object, e.g. 'Is it to the right of 1?' Encourage the use of to the right/left, next to, near, behind, in front of, between.

Follow instructions

NEEDED
Follow instructions

WHAT TO DO   *(work in pairs – best if students sit back to back)*

One student has a copy of the picture and gives instructions for the partner to produce a copy. Once the copy has been produced, the giving of instructions and accuracy can be discussed. Then the roles are reversed.

Maths the Basic Skills Curriculum Edition: Measures, Shape and Space Worksheet Pack © Nelson Thornes Ltd 2004

Money domino cards

seven pence	**4p**	seven pence	**3p**
nine pence	**7p**	nine pence	**2p**
eight pence	**1p**	eight pence	**5p**
three pence	**3p**	three pence	**4p**
five pence	**2p**	five pence	**7p**
four pence	**5p**	four pence	**8p**
one pence	**8p**	one pence	**9p**
two pence	**10p**	two pence	**6p**
six pence	**9p**	six pence	**10p**
ten pence	**6p**	ten pence	**1p**

Activities

Money dominoes – coins and notes

£20	**20p**
50p	**£1**
£2	**£5**
£10	**10p**
5p	**10p**
1p	

Number cards

1	2	3
4	5	6
7	8	9

0	1	2	3	4
5	6	7	8	9

The smaller cards act as number cards up to 9. From 10 onwards, these cards act as the units, going on top of the larger cards on their right hand side to give any combination up to 99.

To Make cards

52p	41p	34p	27p	22p
17p	16p	13p	8p	6p
£19	£18	£16	£13	£12
£11	£9	£8	£7	£3

Activities

1p	1p	1p	1p	1p
2p	2p	2p	2p	2p
2p	2p	2p	5p	5p
5p	5p	5p	5p	5p
10p	10p	10p	10p	10p
20p	20p	20p	20p	20p
£1	£1	£1	£1	£1
£1	£1	£1	£1	£1
£2	£2	£2	£2	£2
£2	£2	£2	£5	£5
£5	£5	£5	£5	£10
£10	£10	£10	£10	£10

10p	20p	30p
40p	50p	60p
70p	80p	90p

Activities

£1	£2	£3
£4	£5	£6
£7	£8	£9
£10	£11	£12
£13	£14	£15
£16	£17	£18
£19	£20	

Jan 02	09 January	January 04
Mar 01	07 December	June August
Nov June	March 05	February 03
Oct February	Apr March	April 06
November April	May Sep	May September
August 11	Jun May	July 10
Dec July	Aug November	December 08
September 12	Feb October	October Jul

Activities

Activities

05:00	11:00	05:30	11:30	02:45	05:45	08:45	11:45
04:00	10:00	04:30	10:30	02:15	05:15	08:15	11:15
03:00	09:00	03:30	09:30	01:45	04:45	07:45	10:45
02:00	08:00	02:30	08:30	01:15	04:15	07:15	10:15
01:00	07:00	01:30	07:30	00:45	03:45	06:45	09:45
00:00	06:00	00:30	06:30	00:15	03:15	06:15	09:15

1 hour	2 hours	3 hours
4 hours	5 hours	6 hours
7 hours	8 hours	9 hours
10 hours	11 hours	12 hours
Half an hour	Quarter of an hour	Three quarters of an hour

Activities

Activities

bigger	larger
smaller	biggest
largest	smallest

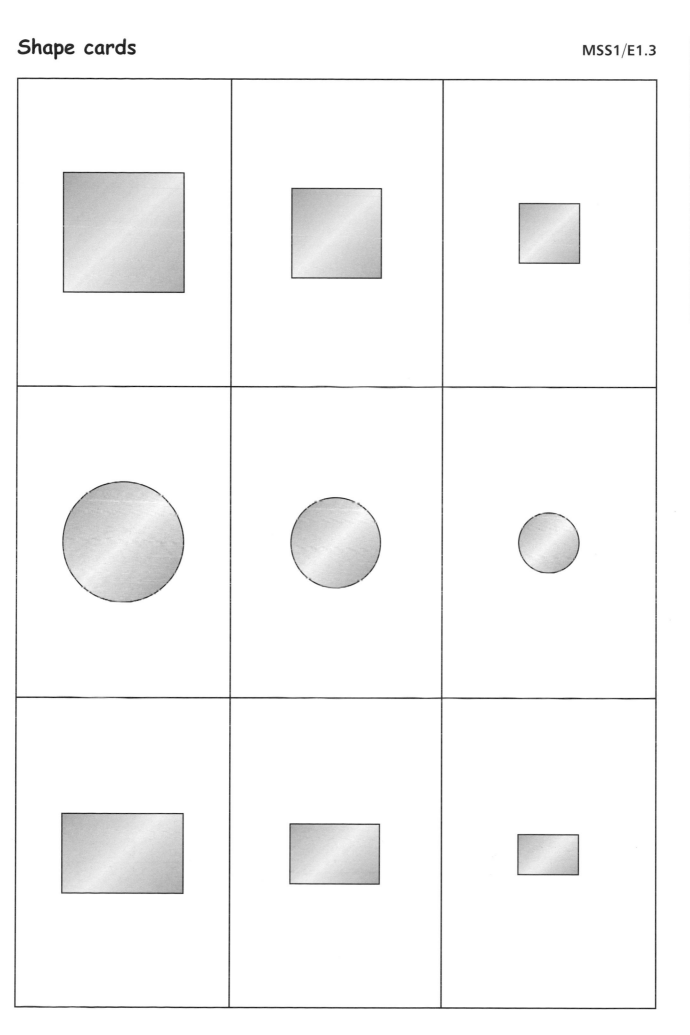

Activities

Activities

wider	taller	thinner
widest	narrower	thinnest
shorter	longest	tall
shortest	longer	tallest

Maths the Basic Skills Curriculum Edition: Measures, Shape and Space Worksheet Pack © Nelson Thornes Ltd 2004

Activities

Weight cards

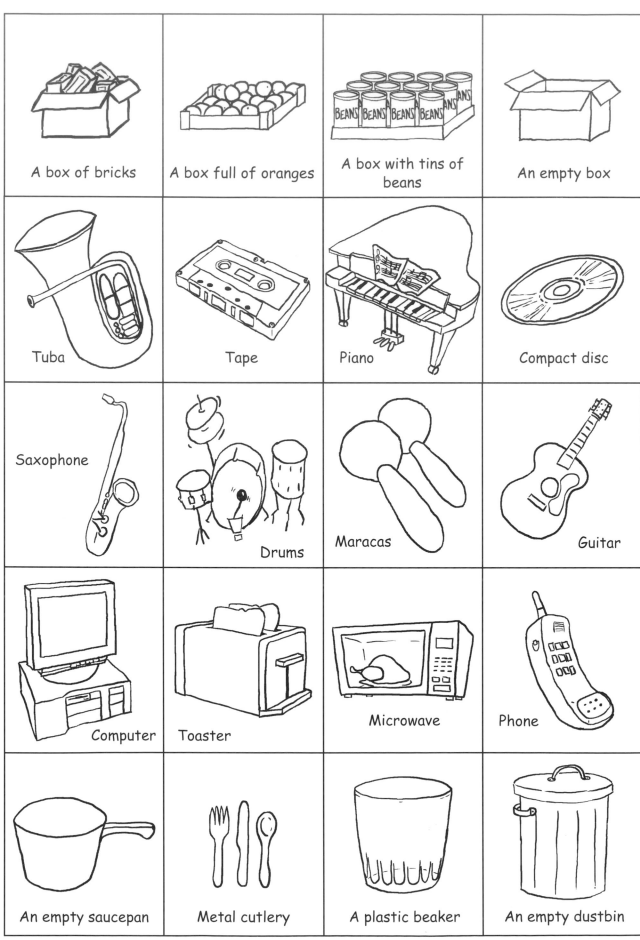

A box of bricks	A box full of oranges	A box with tins of beans	An empty box
Tuba	Tape	Piano	Compact disc
Saxophone	Drums	Maracas	Guitar
Computer	Toaster	Microwave	Phone
An empty saucepan	Metal cutlery	A plastic beaker	An empty dustbin

Activities

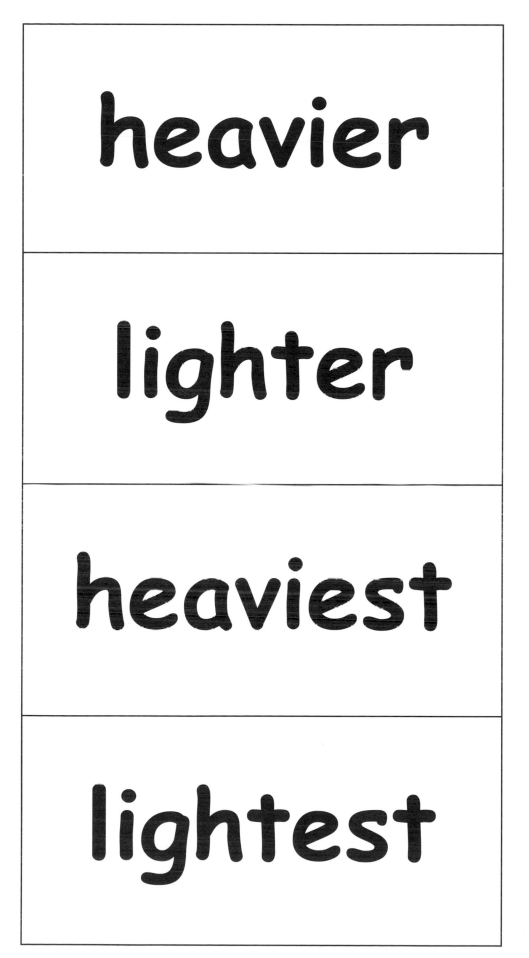

heavier

lighter

heaviest

lightest

Activities

Empty	Full
holds least	holds most
holds less than	holds more than

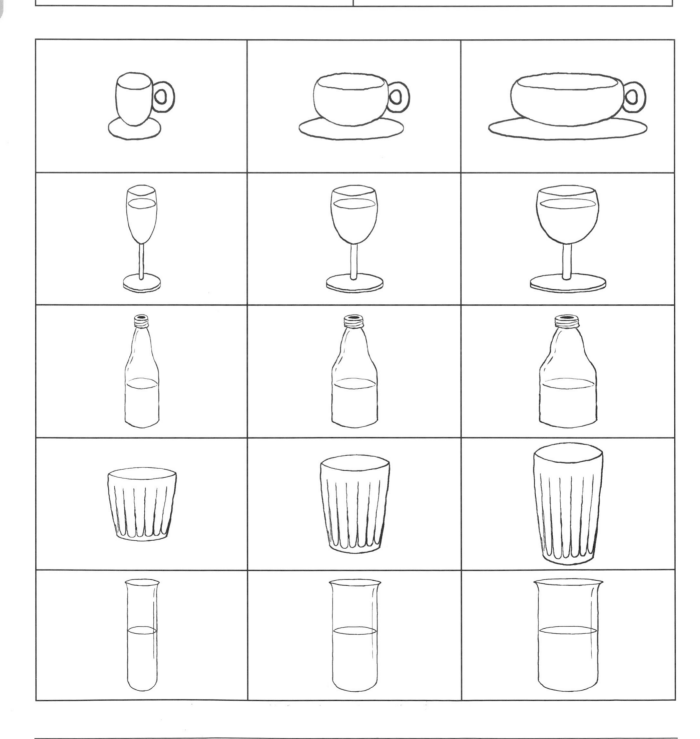

MSS2/E2.3

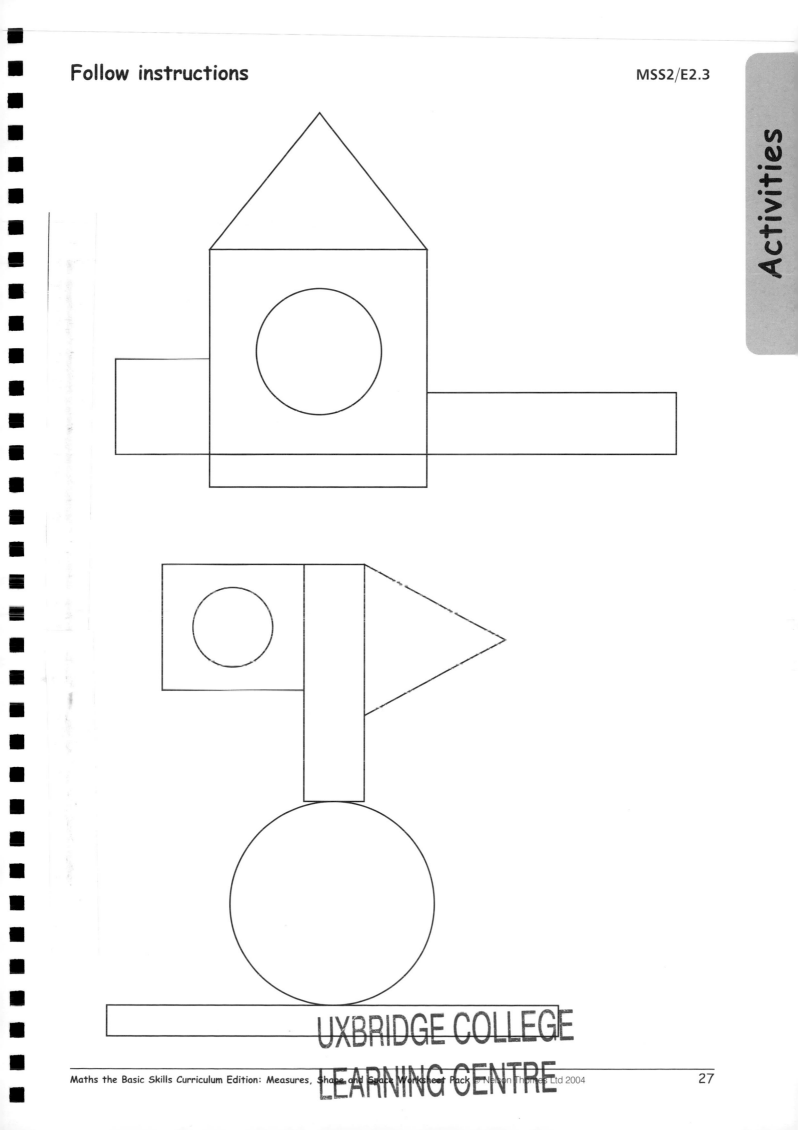

Activities

Choose coins

5p   £1   £2   20p

2p   50p   10p   1p

Which coins do you need?

Tea   20p
Coffee   30p

A cup of tea

£2 per wash

One wash

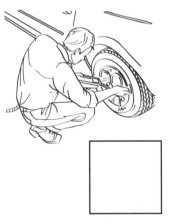

10p for air

phone

Local short call
20p

Worksheets

Put the coins in order

Put the coins in order with the **smallest** value first.

Put the coins in order with the **largest** value first.

Which coins are missing from this list?

Worksheets

Match the £s

Draw a line to match the value with the coins and notes.

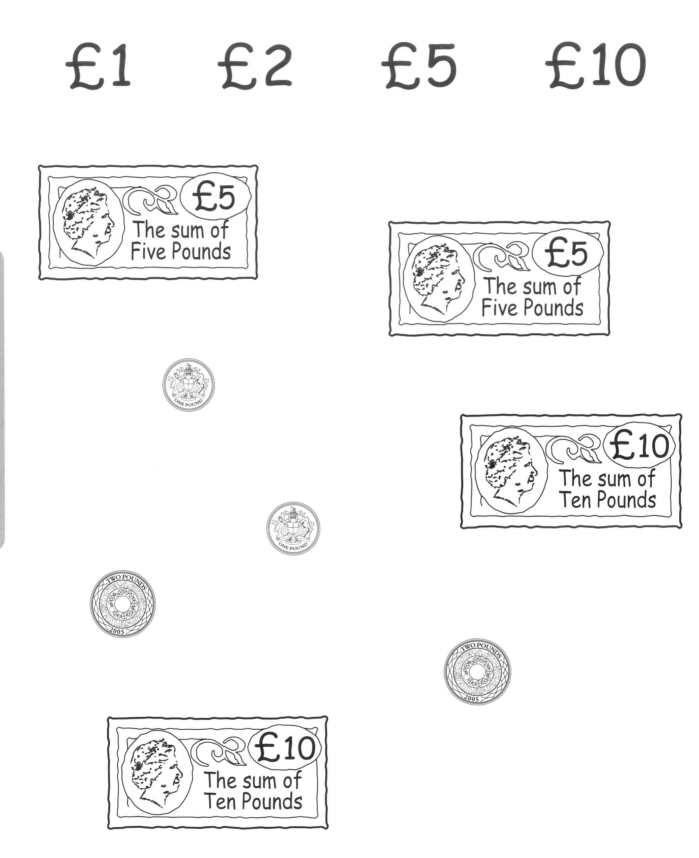

£1   £2   £5   £10

Worksheets

Which coin or note?

You need a selection of £1 and £2 coins, £5, £10 and £20 notes.

Draw a line to the correct answer.

Which coin or note is worth £1?

Which coin or note is worth £2?

Which note is worth £5?

Which note is worth £10?

Which note is worth £20?

Which coin or note is worth the most? _____

Which coin or note is worth the least? _____

Write the notes and coins in order of value

Worth most   Worth least

_____   _____   _____   _____   _____

Worksheets

Find the value – up to 10p

MSS1/E1.1

You need a selection of coins.

Select the coins shown in each box.

Write the total of the coins in the circle.

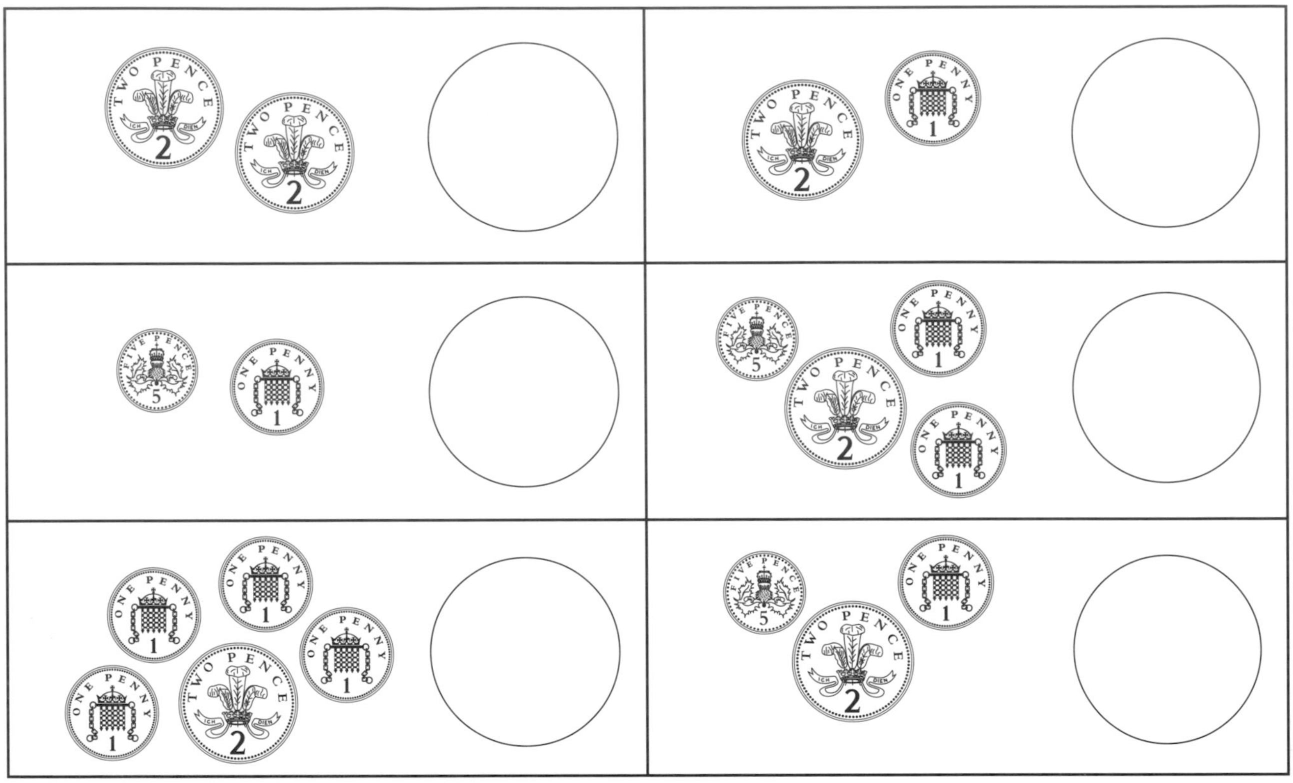

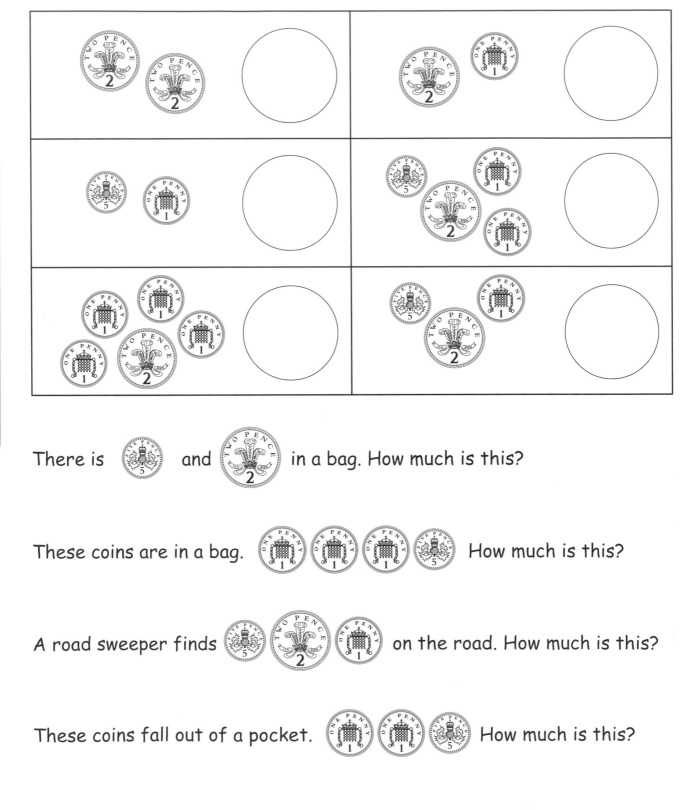

There is  and  in a bag. How much is this?

These coins are in a bag.  How much is this?

A road sweeper finds  on the road. How much is this?

These coins fall out of a pocket.  How much is this?

 © Nelson Thornes Ltd 2004

Which coins are in the bag?

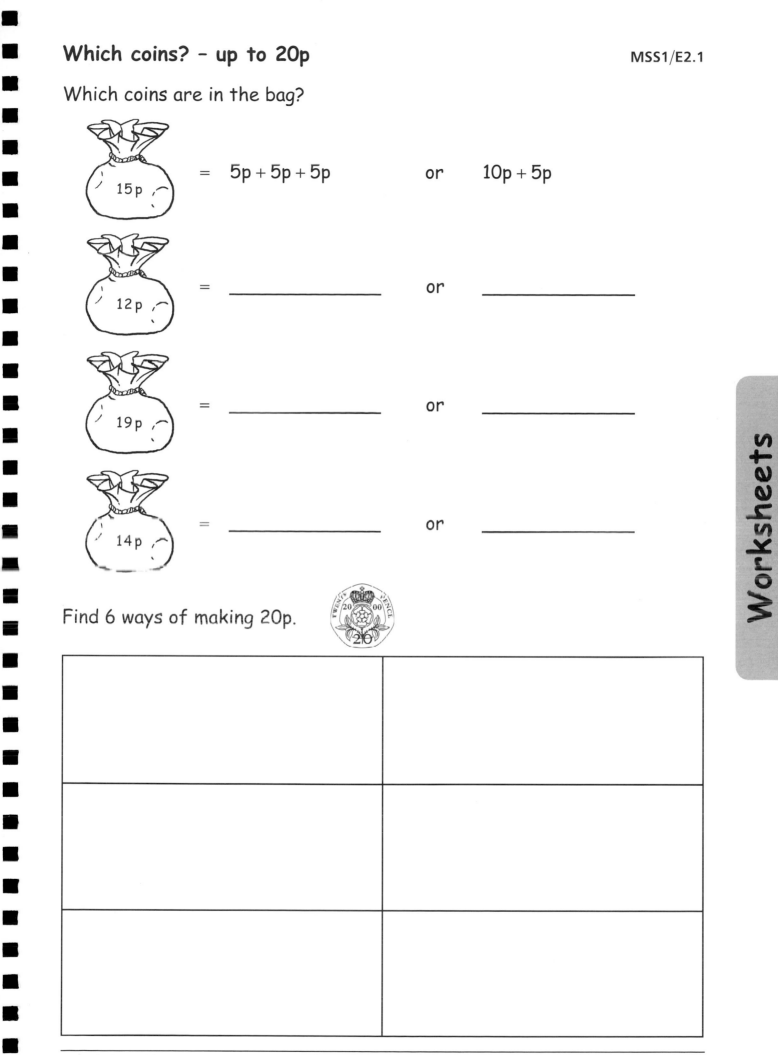

15p   =   5p + 5p + 5p   or   10p + 5p

12p   =   _____   or   _____

19p   =   _____   or   _____

14p   =   _____   or   _____

Find 6 ways of making 20p.

Worksheets

Find 6 ways of making 50p.

<table>
<tr><td></td><td></td></tr>
<tr><td></td><td></td></tr>
<tr><td></td><td></td></tr>
</table>

Each box of coins has the same value as a single coin. Find the coin.
The first is done for you.

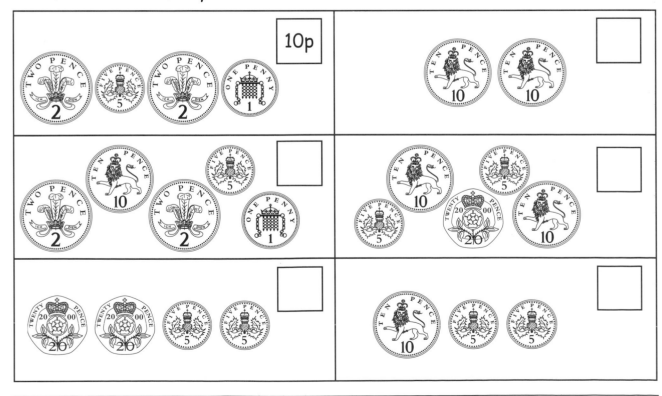

 Maths the Basic Skills Curriculum Edition: Measures, Shape and Space Worksheet Pack © Nelson Thornes Ltd 2004

Which coins?

You need a selection of coins.

Which coins do you need?

20p = 20p   or   10p + 10p   or   _____

80p = _____   or   _____   or   _____

60p = _____   or   _____   or   _____

70p = _____   or   _____   or   _____

40p = _____   or   _____   or   _____

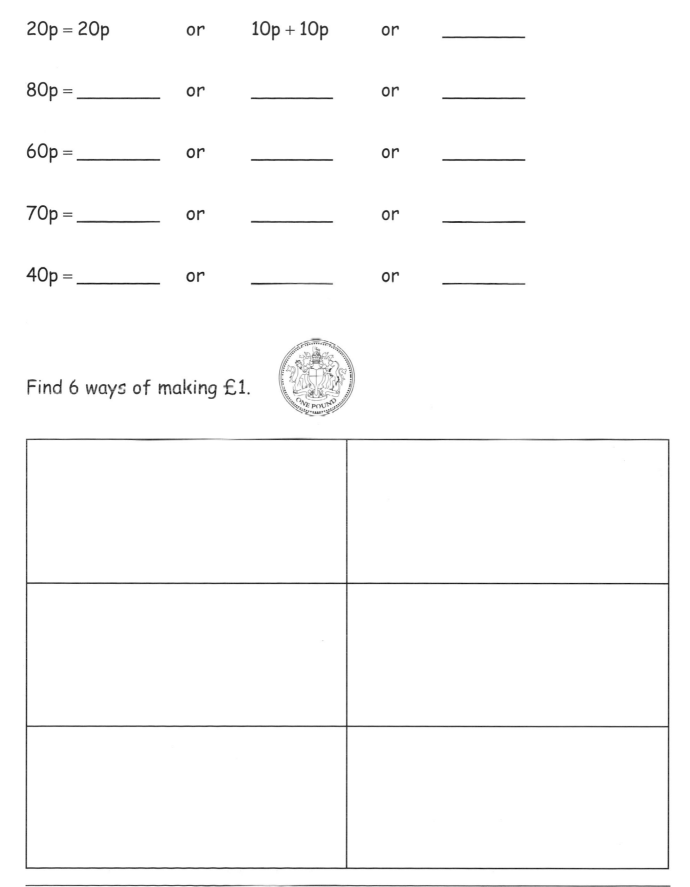

Find 6 ways of making £1.

<table>
<tr><td></td><td></td></tr>
<tr><td></td><td></td></tr>
<tr><td></td><td></td></tr>
</table>

Worksheets

Which coins can you use to pay for each item?

Newspaper 36p	**Bag of chips** 99p
Packet of biscuits 76p	**Cup of tea** 45p
Bottle of pop 85p	**Tin of beans** 22p

What **extra** coins do you need to make the value in each box?
The first is done for you.

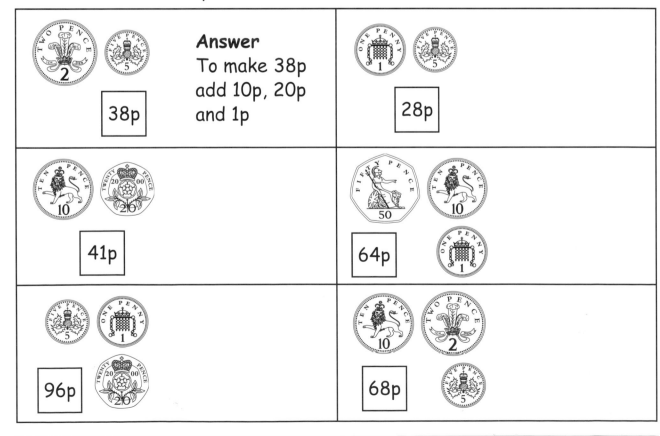

Answer
To make 38p add 10p, 20p and 1p

38p

28p

41p

64p

96p

68p

Maths the Basic Skills Curriculum Edition: Measures, Shape and Space Worksheet Pack © Nelson Thornes Ltd 2004

Shop with £1 – Part A

You need a selection of coins.

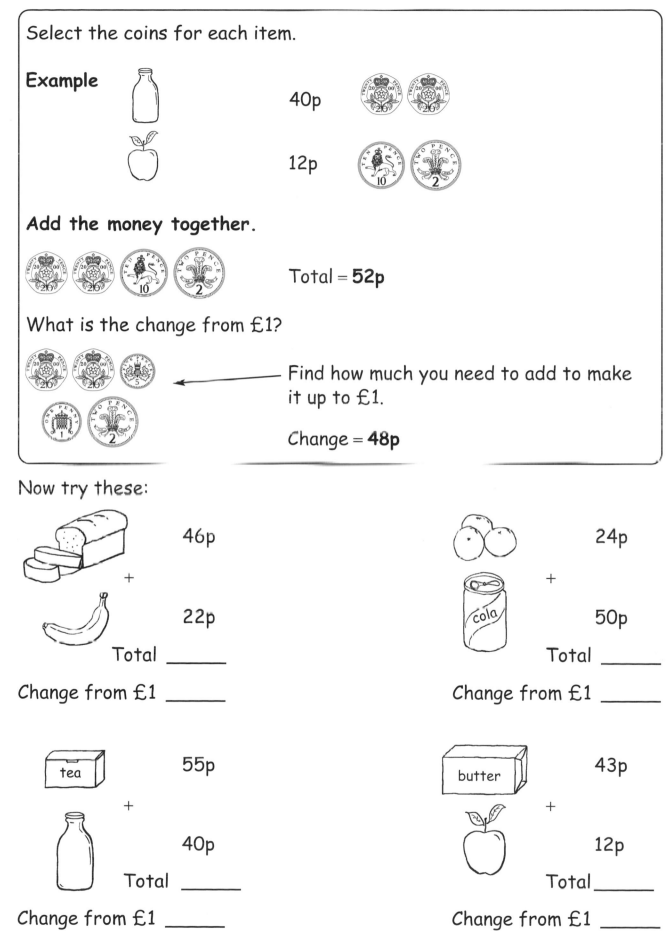

Select the coins for each item.

Example

🍾 40p

🍎 12p

Add the money together.

Total = **52p**

What is the change from £1?

Find how much you need to add to make it up to £1.

Change = **48p**

Now try these:

bread	46p
+ banana	22p
Total _____	
Change from £1 _____	

oranges	24p
+ cola	50p
Total _____	
Change from £1 _____	

tea	55p
+ milk	40p
Total _____	
Change from £1 _____	

butter	43p
+ apple	12p
Total _____	
Change from £1 _____	

Worksheets

Bread	35p	Crisps	25p	Chocolate	42p
Tea	42p	Pear	12p	Crisps	25p
Apple	12p	Coke	50p	Apple	12p

| Total | _____ | Total | _____ | Total | _____ |

| Change | _____ | Change | _____ | Change | _____ |

Spaghetti	32p	Pear	12p	Beans	16p
Sauce	56p	Peach	23p	Bread	30p
Tomato	10p	Cheese	42p	Banana	22p

| Total | _____ | Total | _____ | Total | _____ |

| Change | _____ | Change | _____ | Change | _____ |

Try the rest on paper:

1   Two peaches cost 24p each. You give the shopkeeper 50p.
    What change should you get?

2   A banana costs 25p and a peach costs 24p. What is the change
    from 50p?

3   A peach costs 15p and a can of cola costs 40p.
    How much do they cost altogether? What change is there from £1?

4   Potatoes cost 32p, carrots 22p and a cabbage 40p.
    How much do they cost altogether? What is the change from £1?

5   Ice creams are 42p each. You buy two. How much do they cost
    altogether?
    How much change is there from £1?

6   A can of beans costs 22p, bread 35p and an apple 22p.
    What is the total cost? How much change is there from £1?

You need a selection of coins.

Select the correct money for each item.
Put the coins together.
Exchange some coins for a 10p if you can.
Add the coins together.

Example

Milk   39p

Sugar   55p

Exchange the two 5p coins for one 10p coin.

Total = **94p**

What change is there from £1?      Change = **6p**

(Find what you need to add to make £1.)

Carrots	27p	Cabbage	44p	Leeks	35p
Cabbage	35p	Potatoes	39p	Carrots	26p
Total	_____	Total	_____	Total	_____
Change	_____	Change	_____	Change	_____

Tomatoes	36p	Pasta	55p	Beans	24p
Onions	17p	Pepper	37p	Soup	39p
Total	_____	Total	_____	Total	_____
Change	_____	Change	_____	Change	_____

Worksheets

Shopping

| Bread | 35p |
| Peach | 25p |

Total _____

Change _____
from £1

| Tomatoes | 35p |
| Spaghetti | 29p |

Total _____

Change _____
from £1

| Bread | 36p |
| Onions | 17p |

Total _____

Change _____
from £1

Soup	36p
Bread	27p
Butter	34p

Total _____

Change _____
from £1

Beans	26p
Tomatoes	25p
Bread	35p

Total _____

Change _____
from £1

Carrots	31p
Pepper	25p
Mushrooms	29p

Total _____

Change _____
from £1

Try the rest on paper:

1 Crisps cost 29p and a can of drink costs 42p. What is the total cost?
How much change is there from £1?

2 A chocolate bar costs 38p and a newspaper costs 35p.
How much is this altogether? How much change is there from £1?

3 Two toffee chews cost 14p each. How much is this?
How much change is there from 50p?

4 A magazine costs 55p and a bar of chocolate is 38p.
How much is this altogether? How much change is there from £1?

5 Sweets cost 24p and a newspaper costs 38p.
How much is this altogether?
What change is there from £1?

6 A toffee bar costs 14p and crisps cost 28p.
How much is this altogether?
How much change is there from 50p?

Worksheets

Calculate with whole £s

Find the cost of the shopping.
Find the change from £20.

Ruler set	£3	Pad and pen set	£4	Gel pen set	£6
Pad and pen set	£4	Marker pen set	£5	Ruler set	£3
Felt pen set	£7	Gel pen set	£6	Twin pens	£2

| Total | _____ | Total | _____ | Total | _____ |
| Change | _____ | Change | _____ | Change | _____ |

Try the rest on paper:

1 It costs £4 to go to the gym. A swim costs £2 extra. A meal costs £6.
   How much is this altogether?
   The sports player pays for it with a £20 note.
   How much change will she get?

2 Three friends go to a nightclub. It costs £6 each to get in.
   How much do they have left from £20?

3 Two drinks cost £3 each and a third costs £2. These are paid for with
   a £10 note. Is there enough left to buy a large bag of crisps for £1?

4 Look at the price list.

chips £1   burger £2   pizza £6   cake £3   super fruit £5

Find the missing items:

a Raj spends £3 on _____ and _____

b Mick spends £4 on _____ and _____

c Bill spends £5 on _____ and _____

d Yui spends £6 on _____ and _____

e Ann spends £9 on _____ and _____

Worksheets

The little hand tells us the hour.
The big hand tells us the minutes.
If the big hand is on the 12, it means **o'clock**.

3 o'clock

7 o'clock

What is the time?

Draw the hands to show:

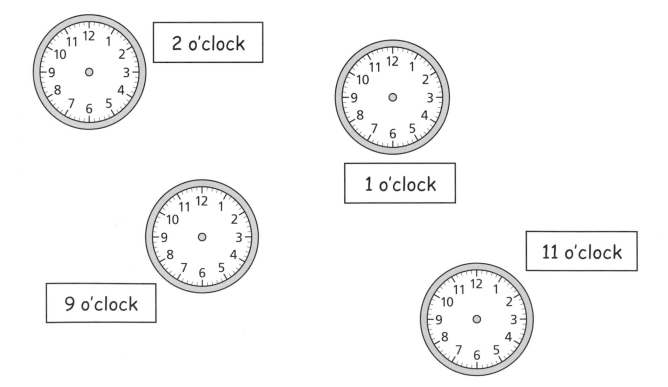

2 o'clock

1 o'clock

9 o'clock

11 o'clock

What were you doing today or what will you do at these times?	
morning	6 o'clock
	7 o'clock
	8 o'clock
	9 o'clock
	10 o'clock
	11 o'clock
	12 o'clock midday
afternoon	1 o'clock
	2 o'clock
	3 o'clock
	4 o'clock
	5 o'clock
evening	6 o'clock
	7 o'clock
	8 o'clock
	9 o'clock
	10 o'clock
	11 o'clock
	12 o'clock midnight

Worksheets

Worksheets

Plan your weekly activities. When will you do the shopping? When are you at college?

Days	Morning am	12 o'clock midday	Afternoon pm	Evening pm	12 o'clock midnight Most of us sleep			
Sunday								Weekend
Monday								
Tuesday								
Wednesday								
Thursday								
Friday								
Saturday								Weekend

Write the date

	Month	Abbreviated
1	January	Jan
2	February	Feb
3	March	Mar
4	April	Apr
5	May	May
6	June	Jun
7	July	Jul
8	August	Aug
9	September	Sep
10	October	Oct
11	November	Nov
12	December	Dec

There are different ways to write the date.

Full date	16th November 2002
Medium date	16/Nov/2002

Use the abbreviated month.

Short date	16/11/02

November is the 11th month

This means 2002.

1 Add your family birthdays to the chart. Use the short date format.

2 Do you have any special events at home, e.g. holidays planned?
   Add these in the full date format.

3 Add Christmas Day and Easter Day to the chart.
   Use the medium date format.

January/2_ _ _	
February	
March	
April	
May	
June	
July	
August	
September	
October	
November	
December	

Worksheets

Match the dates

Draw lines to match the dates.

1st January 2004	21/Jun/2004	15/03/04
28th February 2004	10/Aug/2004	17/04/04
16th October 2004	1/Jul/2004	16/10/04
31st July 2004	1/Jan/2004	21/05/04
21st May 2004	25/Dec/2004	17/09/04
17th September 2004	5/Nov/2004	31/07/04
5th November 2004	15/Mar/2004	10/12/04
10th December 2004	17/Apr/2004	1/07/04
15th March 2004	10/Dec/2004	28/02/04
1st July 2004	31/Jul/2004	25/12/04
21st June 2004	28/Feb/2004	21/06/04
25th December 2004	16/Oct/2004	5/11/04
10th August 2004	21/May/2004	10/08/04
17th April 2004	17/Sep/2004	1/01/04

Worksheets

1 a You buy a new TV on the date shown on the calendar.
  What is the date on your receipt?

February 2003   Write your answers in the boxes.

S	M	T	W	T	F	S
1	2	3	4	5	6	7
8	9	10	11	12	13	14
15	16	17	18	19	20	21
22	23	24	25	26	27	28

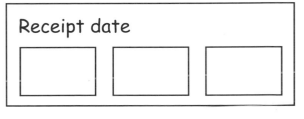

Receipt date

b You have a guarantee for 10 months.
  In which month does the guarantee run out?

c You call the engineer out to mend the TV on the date shown on the
  calendar below. What is the date?

October 2003   Call out date

S	M	T	W	T	F	S
			1	2	3	4
5	6	7	8	9	10	11
12	13	14	15	16	17	18
19	20	21	22	23	24	25
26	27	28	29	30	31	

d Can you have the TV mended under the guarantee?

2 You fill in a registration card for a library ticket.
  Fill in the date shown on the calendar.

January 2004   Ticket start date

S	M	T	W	T	F	S
				1	2	3
4	5	6	7	8	9	10
11	12	13	14	15	16	17
18	19	20	21	22	23	24
25	26	27	28	29	30	31

All these clocks say **9 o'clock**.

Analogue clocks

Digital clock

hours   minutes

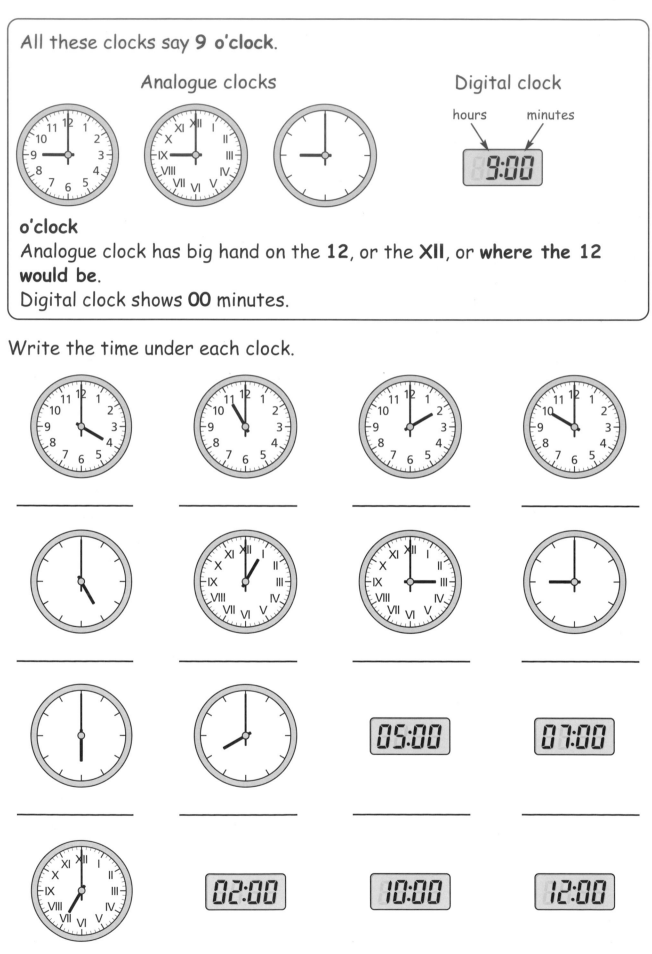

o'clock

Analogue clock has big hand on the **12**, or the **XII**, or **where the 12 would be**.

Digital clock shows **00** minutes.

Write the time under each clock.

Worksheets

All these clocks say **half past 9**, or **nine thirty**, or **9:30**.

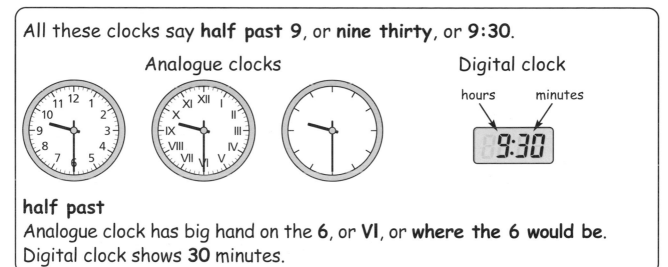

Analogue clocks

Digital clock

hours   minutes

half past
Analogue clock has big hand on the **6**, or **VI**, or **where the 6 would be**.
Digital clock shows **30** minutes.

Write the time under each clock in all 3 ways.
The first is done for you.

half past 2
two thirty
2:30

_____
_____
_____

_____
_____
_____

_____
_____
_____

_____
_____
_____

_____
_____
_____

_____
_____
_____

_____
_____
_____

_____
_____
_____

_____
_____
_____

_____
_____
_____

_____
_____
_____

_____
_____
_____

Worksheets

Match the times

Draw lines between the times that match.

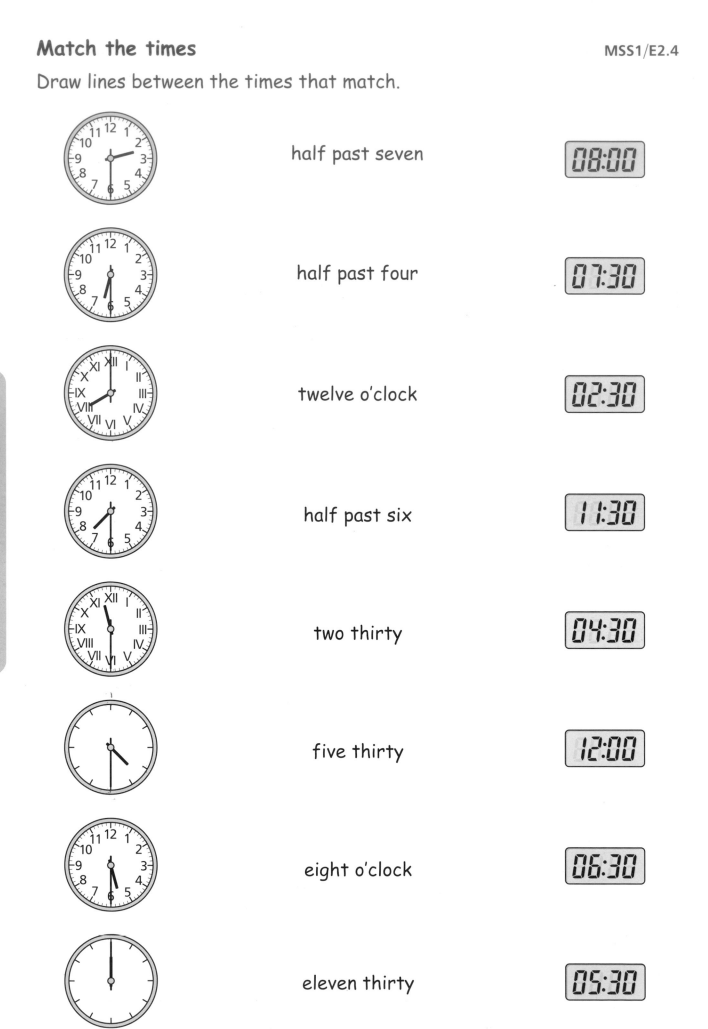

half past seven

08:00

half past four

07:30

twelve o'clock

02:30

half past six

11:30

two thirty

04:30

five thirty

12:00

eight o'clock

06:30

eleven thirty

05:30

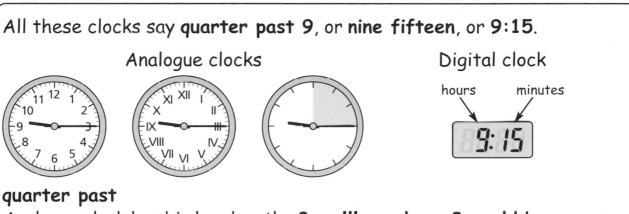

All these clocks say **quarter past 9**, or **nine fifteen**, or **9:15**.

Analogue clocks

Digital clock

hours   minutes

quarter past

Analogue clock has big hand on the **3**, or **III**, or **where 3 would be**.

Digital clock shows **15** minutes.

Write the time under each clock in all 3 ways.

The first is done for you.

quarter past 2
two fifteen
2:15

_____

_____

_____

_____

_____

_____

_____

_____

_____

_____

_____

_____

_____

_____

_____

_____

_____

_____

_____

_____

_____

_____

_____

Worksheets

Quarter past

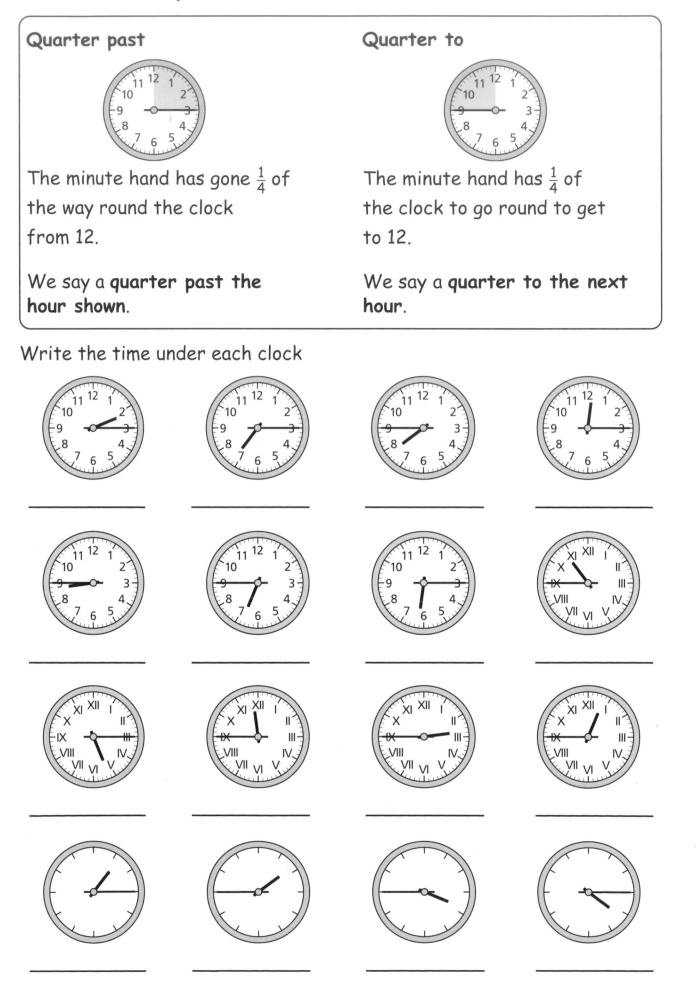

The minute hand has gone $\frac{1}{4}$ of the way round the clock from 12.

We say a **quarter past the hour shown**.

Quarter to

The minute hand has $\frac{1}{4}$ of the clock to go round to get to 12.

We say a **quarter to the next hour**.

Write the time under each clock

_____ _____ _____ _____

_____ _____ _____ _____

_____ _____ _____ _____

_____ _____ _____ _____

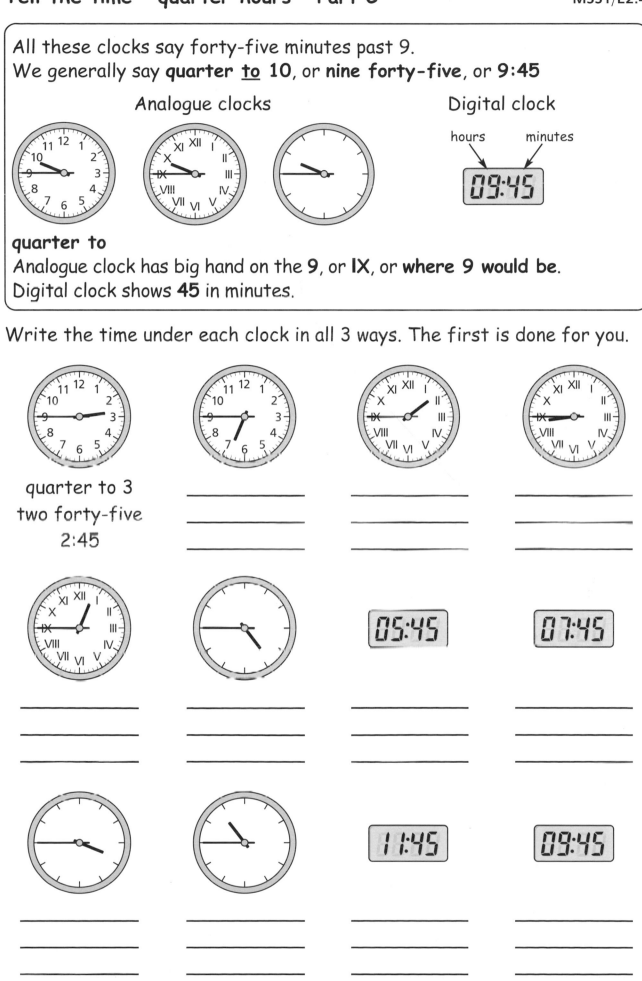

All these clocks say forty-five minutes past 9.
We generally say **quarter <u>to</u> 10**, or **nine forty-five**, or **9:45**

Analogue clocks   Digital clock

hours   minutes

quarter to
Analogue clock has big hand on the **9**, or **IX**, or **where 9 would be.**
Digital clock shows **45** in minutes.

Write the time under each clock in all 3 ways. The first is done for you.

quarter to 3
two forty-five
2:45

05:45   07:45

11:45   09:45

Worksheets

Draw lines between the times that match.

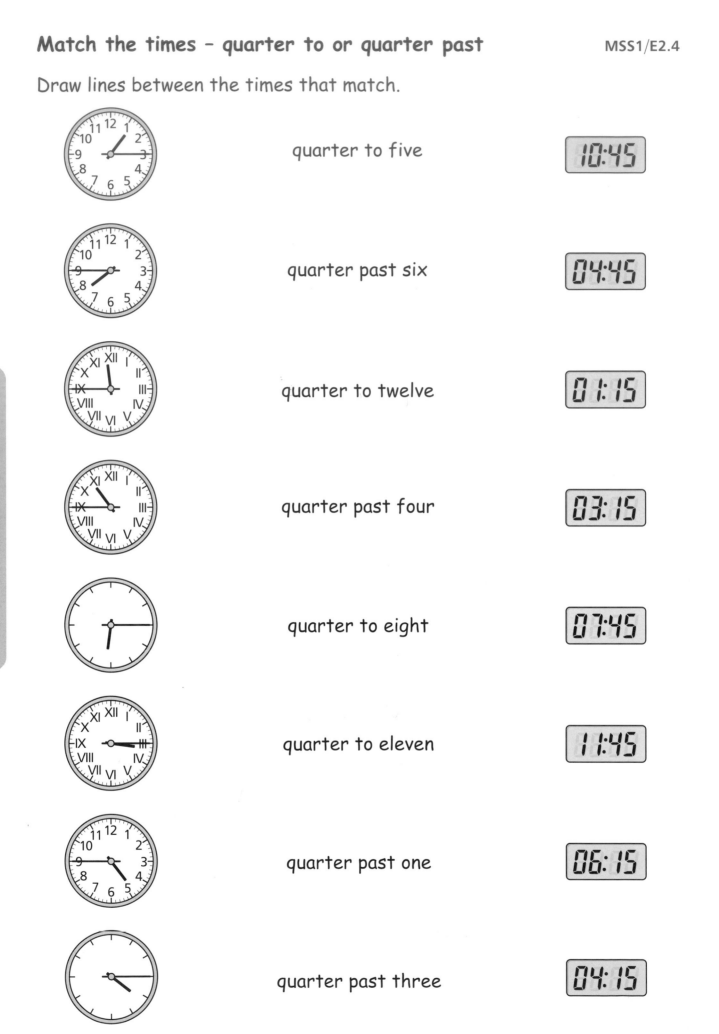

quarter to five

`10:45`

quarter past six

`04:45`

quarter to twelve

`01:15`

quarter past four

`03:15`

quarter to eight

`07:45`

quarter to eleven

`11:45`

quarter past one

`06:15`

quarter past three

`04:15`

Find the time

1 Your class starts at 10:30:

   You watch shows this time.

   Has your class started yet? _____

2 You get a video. The video is $2\frac{1}{2}$ hours long.

   You start watching the video at: `08:00`

   When does the video end? _____

3 You go to the gym at:

   You stay at the gym for half an hour.

   When do you leave the gym? Write the time on a digital watch.   `88:88`

4 You get home at: `06:45`

   Your sister promised to call at quarter past six.

   Are you in time for your sister's call? _____

5 You are at the bus stop at: `09:15`

   The bus arrives at half past nine. Will you catch the bus? _____

6 You work 4 hours on a Saturday. You start work at:

   When do you stop working? _____

7 A football match starts at quarter to eight.

   Your watch says: `07:30`

   Are you in time for the start of the match? _____

Worksheets

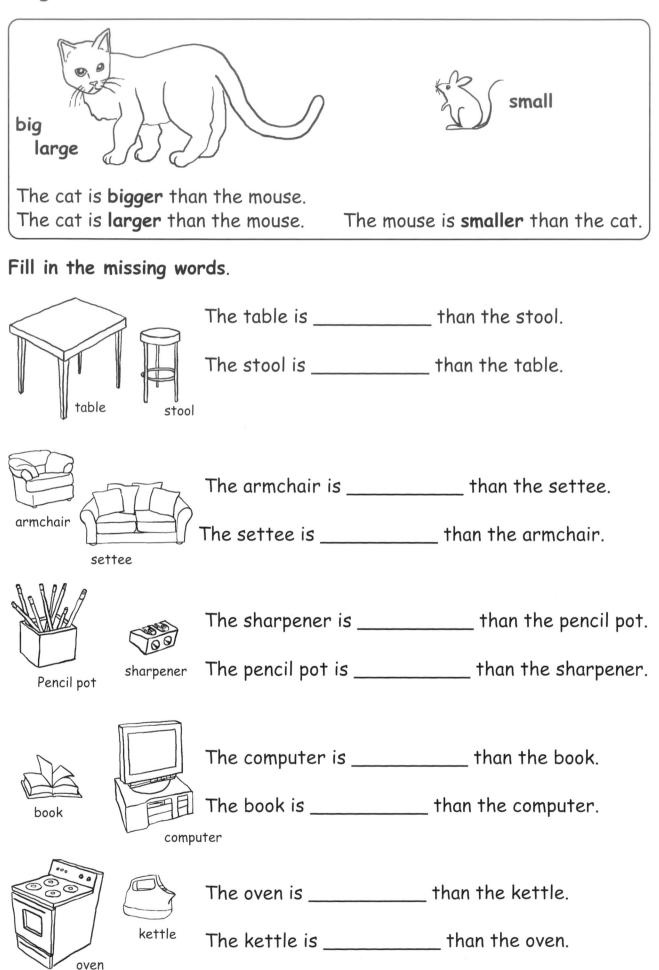

big
large

small

The cat is **bigger** than the mouse.
The cat is **larger** than the mouse.   The mouse is **smaller** than the cat.

Fill in the missing words.

table   stool

The table is _____ than the stool.

The stool is _____ than the table.

armchair

settee

The armchair is _____ than the settee.

The settee is _____ than the armchair.

Pencil pot   sharpener

The sharpener is _____ than the pencil pot.

The pencil pot is _____ than the sharpener.

book

computer

The computer is _____ than the book.

The book is _____ than the computer.

kettle

oven

The oven is _____ than the kettle.

The kettle is _____ than the oven.

Worksheets

Largest or smallest

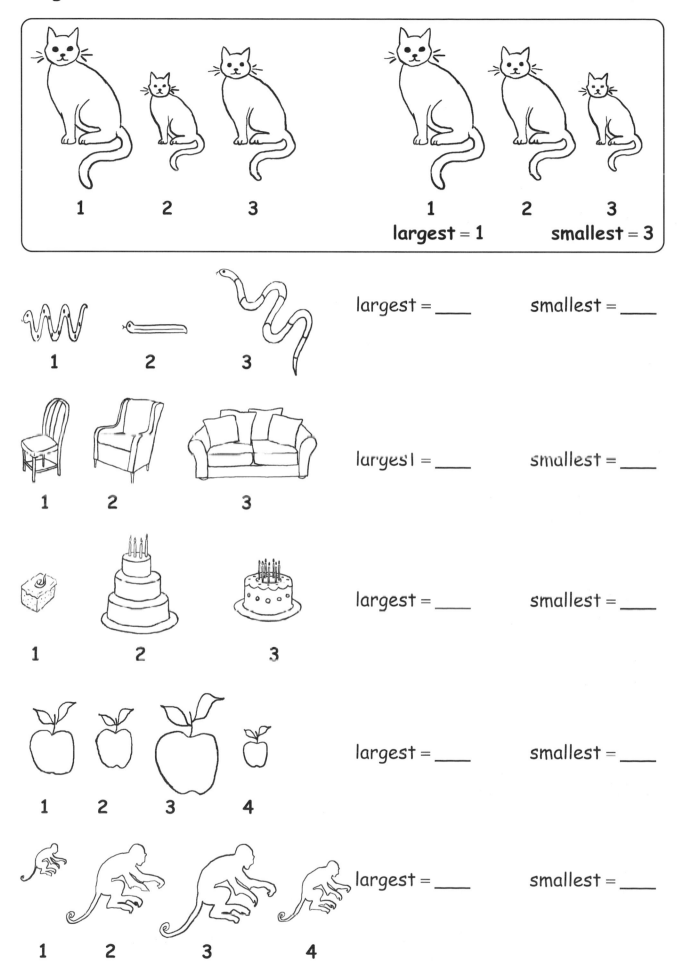

largest = 1   smallest = 3

largest = ___   smallest = ___

largest = ___   smallest = ___

largest = ___   smallest = ___

largest = ___   smallest = ___

largest = ___   smallest = ___

Worksheets

WIDE

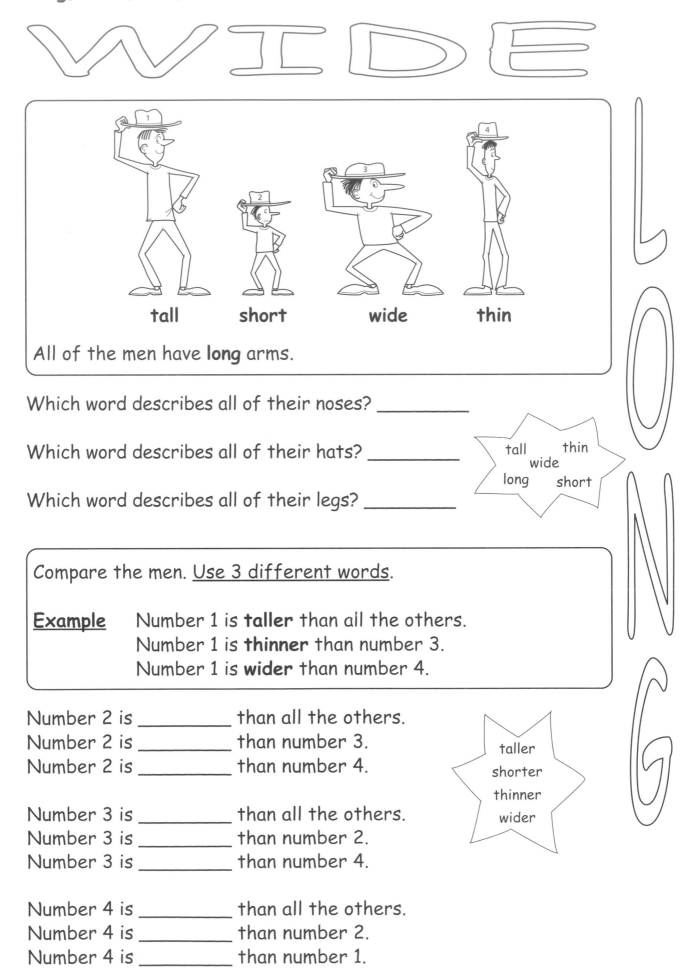

| tall | short | wide | thin |

All of the men have **long** arms.

Which word describes all of their noses? _____

Which word describes all of their hats? _____

Which word describes all of their legs? _____

tall   thin
wide
long   short

Compare the men. <u>Use 3 different words</u>.

<u>Example</u>   Number 1 is **taller** than all the others.
Number 1 is **thinner** than number 3.
Number 1 is **wider** than number 4.

Number 2 is _____ than all the others.
Number 2 is _____ than number 3.
Number 2 is _____ than number 4.

Number 3 is _____ than all the others.
Number 3 is _____ than number 2.
Number 3 is _____ than number 4.

Number 4 is _____ than all the others.
Number 4 is _____ than number 2.
Number 4 is _____ than number 1.

taller
shorter
thinner
wider

Worksheets

LONG

Longer, shorter, wider, narrower

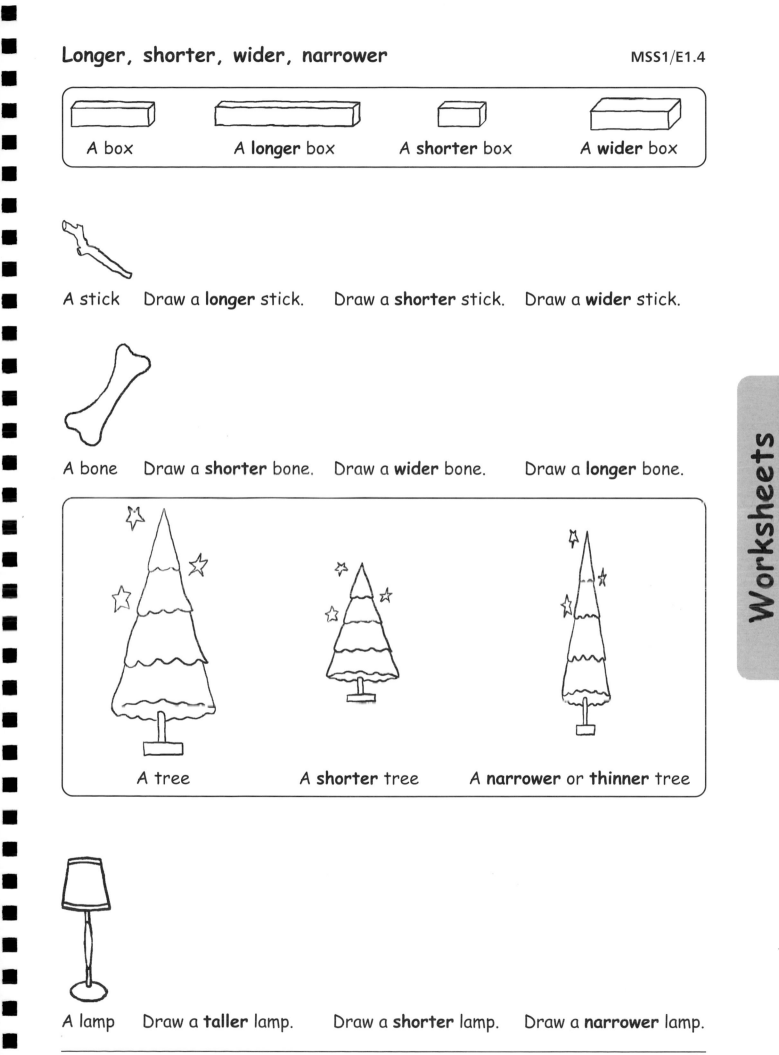

A box   A **longer** box   A **shorter** box   A **wider** box

A stick   Draw a **longer** stick.   Draw a **shorter** stick.   Draw a **wider** stick.

A bone   Draw a **shorter** bone.   Draw a **wider** bone.   Draw a **longer** bone.

A tree   A **shorter** tree   A **narrower** or **thinner** tree

A lamp   Draw a **taller** lamp.   Draw a **shorter** lamp.   Draw a **narrower** lamp.

Worksheets

Longest, shortest, widest, narrowest, thinnest

1   2   3

Which ladder is the **tallest**?
_____

Which ladder is the **shortest**?
_____

Which ladder is the **widest**?
_____

1   2   3

Which torch is the **longest**?
_____

Which torch is the **narrowest**?
_____

Which torch is **widest**?
_____

1   2   3

Which hammer is the **thinnest**?
_____

Which hammer is the **longest**?
_____

Which hammer is the **shortest**?
_____

1   2   3

Lamp 1 is the _____.

Lamp 2 is the _____.

Lamp 3 is the _____.

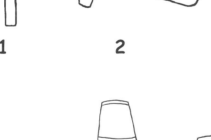

1   2   3

Tail 1 is the _____.

Tail 2 is the _____.

Tail 3 is the _____.

Maths the Basic Skills Curriculum Edition: Measures, Shape and Space Worksheet Pack © Nelson Thornes Ltd 2004

Measure in paces and handspans

A Walk the length of the room. Count the number of paces.
   Record your name and the result in the table.
   Walk the width of the room. Count the number of paces.
   Put the result in the table.

Name	Number of paces for length of the room	Number of paces for width of the room

Ask other people in your group to walk across the room.
Record their results in the table.

B Measure the length and width of the table using hand spans.
   Record your name and the results in the table.
   Ask other people in your group to measure the table using hand spans.
   Record their results.

Name	Number of hand spans	
	length of table	width of table

C Are paces and hand spans an accurate way of measuring things? _____

   Why? _____

Worksheets

Measure in centimetres (cm) – Part A

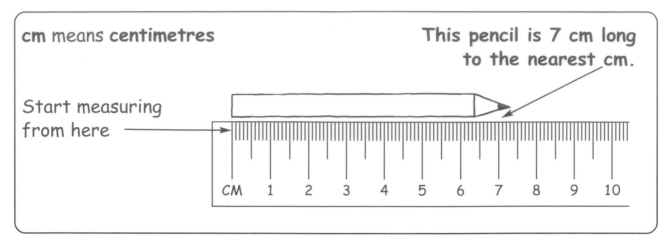

cm means **centimetres**

This pencil is 7 cm long to the nearest cm.

Start measuring from here

CM 1 2 3 4 5 6 7 8 9 10

Measure the length of these lines and objects to the nearest cm.

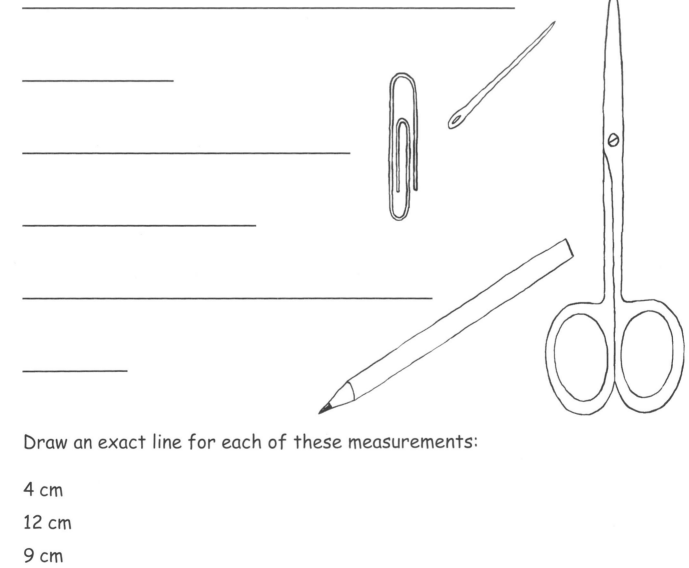

_____

_____

_____

_____

_____

Draw an exact line for each of these measurements:

4 cm

12 cm

9 cm

16 cm

8 cm

Worksheets

Measure in centimetres (cm) – Part B

Measure these shapes **to the nearest cm**.

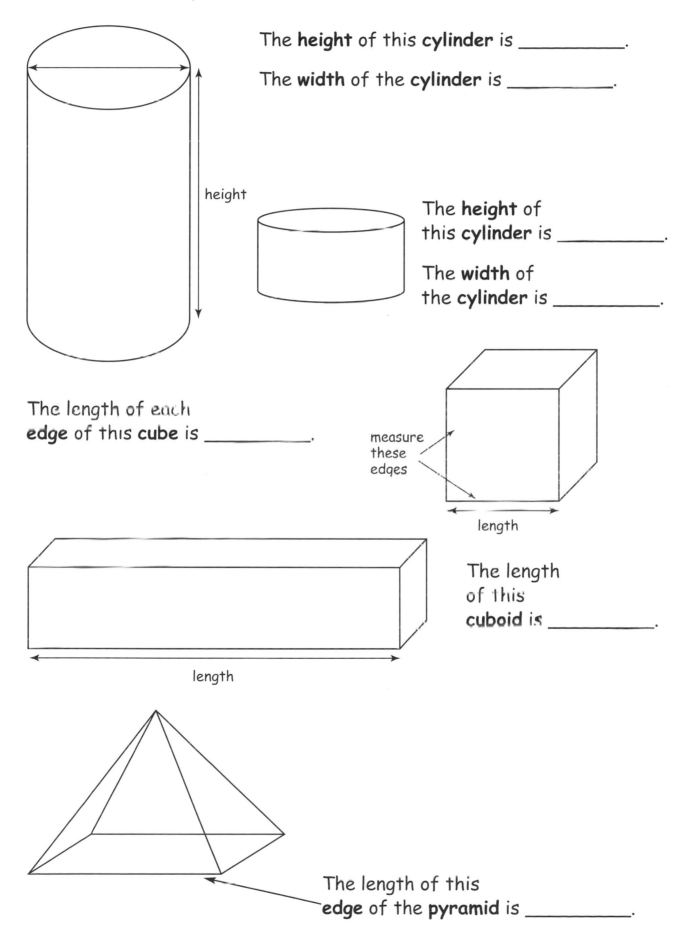

The **height** of this **cylinder** is _____.

The **width** of the **cylinder** is _____.

The **height** of this **cylinder** is _____.

The **width** of the **cylinder** is _____.

height

The length of each **edge** of this **cube** is _____.

measure these edges

length

The length of this **cuboid** is _____.

length

The length of this **edge** of the **pyramid** is _____.

Worksheets

Measure yourself

Measure yourself to the nearest centimetre.

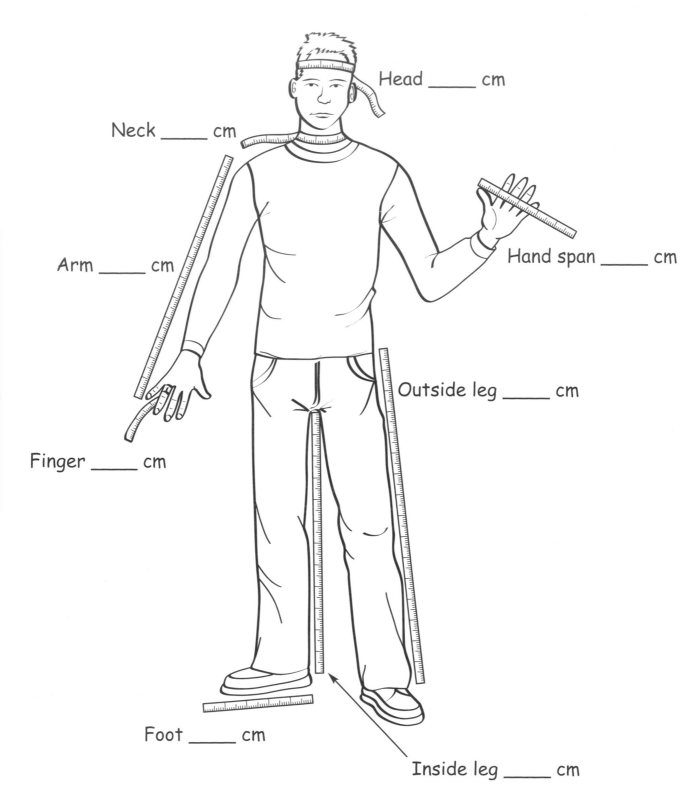

Head _____ cm

Neck _____ cm

Arm _____ cm

Hand span _____ cm

Finger _____ cm

Outside leg _____ cm

Foot _____ cm

Inside leg _____ cm

Worksheets

Maths the Basic Skills Curriculum Edition: Measures, Shape and Space Worksheet Pack © Nelson Thornes Ltd 2004

Measure in metres and centimetres (m and cm)

> Centimetre – cm
>
> —— This line is 1 cm long.
>
> Metre – m
>
> **100 cm = 1 m**

Would you use centimetres or metres to measure these? Write m or cm.

1 The length of the room _____

2 The length of a pencil _____

3 The length of your bed _____

4 The length of a garden _____

5 The length of an envelope _____

6 The width of this paper _____

7 The length of your hand _____

8 The length of a screwdriver _____

9 The height of a door _____

10 The length of a car _____

11 The length of a nail _____

12 The length of a bath _____

Estimate then measure these in metres (m) and centimetres (cm):

	Estimate in metres and centimetres	Accurate measurement in metres and centimetres
Length of table		
Length of room		
Width of room		
Height of the door		
Width of the window		
Your height		

Find four more lengths to measure.

Worksheets

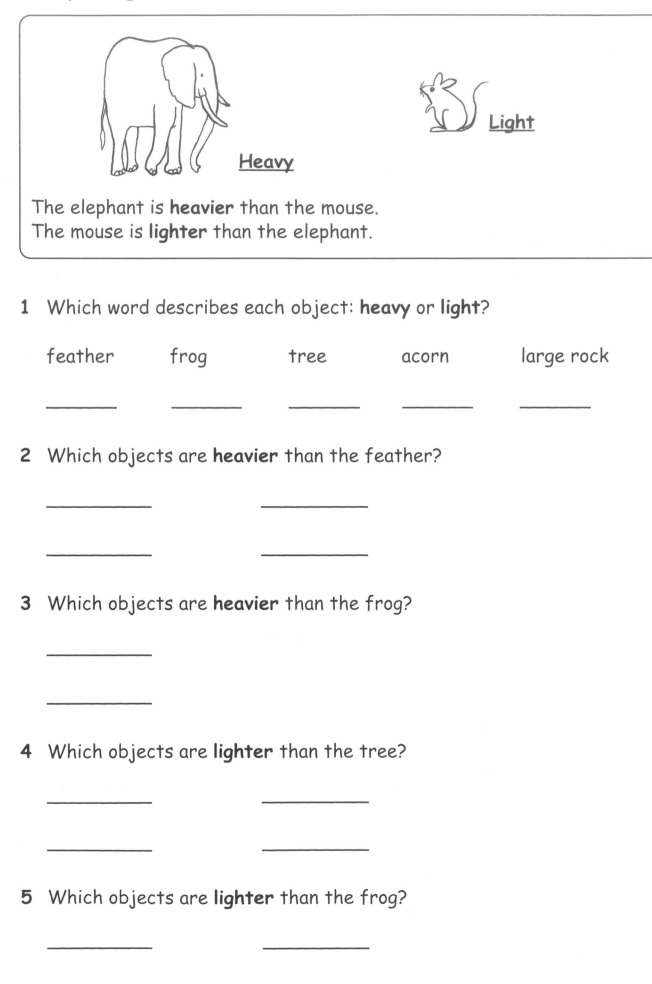

Heavy

Light

The elephant is **heavier** than the mouse.
The mouse is **lighter** than the elephant.

1 Which word describes each object: **heavy** or **light**?

feather   frog   tree   acorn   large rock

_____   _____   _____   _____   _____

2 Which objects are **heavier** than the feather?

_____   _____

_____   _____

3 Which objects are **heavier** than the frog?

_____

_____

4 Which objects are **lighter** than the tree?

_____   _____

_____   _____

5 Which objects are **lighter** than the frog?

_____   _____

Worksheets

Heavier or lighter

You need

Balance scales   Book   Pencil
Bag   Shoe

A 1 Pick up the book.

2 Which objects do you think are **heavier** than the book?

3 Which objects do you think are **lighter** than the book?

4 Fill in the unshaded part of the table. For each object tick a box.

Objects	I think these are **heavier** than the book.	I think these are **lighter** than the book.	I have checked. These are **heavier** than the book.	I have checked. These are **lighter** than the the book.
Pencil				
Bag				
Shoe				

5 Are you right?   Check by: **a** holding the objects
                                      b using the balance scales.

6 Fill in the rest of the table (shaded part).

B 1 Choose another object: pencil, bag or shoe.

2 Say which objects you think are **heavier**.

3 Say which objects you think are **lighter**.

4 Check to see if you are right.

Objects	I think these are **heavier** than the _____.	I think these are **lighter** than the _____.	I have checked. These are **heavier** than the _____.	I have checked. These are **lighter** than the _____.

Worksheets

Heaviest or lightest

Worksheets

Example

Put these in order of weight:

Answer:

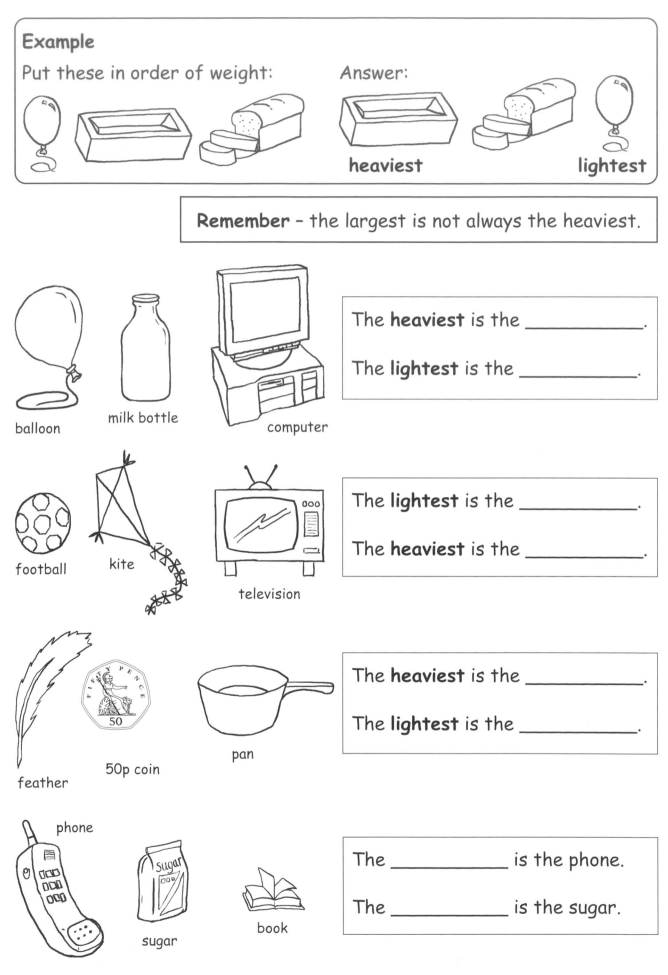

heaviest

lightest

Remember – the largest is not always the heaviest.

The **heaviest** is the _____.

The **lightest** is the _____.

balloon

milk bottle

computer

The **lightest** is the _____.

The **heaviest** is the _____.

football

kite

television

The **heaviest** is the _____.

The **lightest** is the _____.

feather

50p coin

pan

phone

The _____ is the phone.

The _____ is the sugar.

sugar

book

Understand weight in kilograms and grams

Weight is measured in **kilograms (kg)** and **grams (g)**.

A small leaf weighs about 1 g.

A small branch weighs about 1 kg.

Grams are used to measure **light** things.
Kilograms are used to measure **heavy** things.

What would you use to measure these things?   **kilograms** (kg) or **grams** (g)

1

2

3

4

5

6

7

Which is more likely?

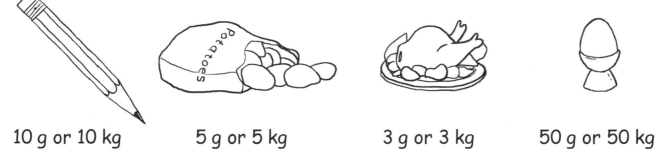

10 g or 10 kg   5 g or 5 kg   3 g or 3 kg   50 g or 50 kg

Worksheets

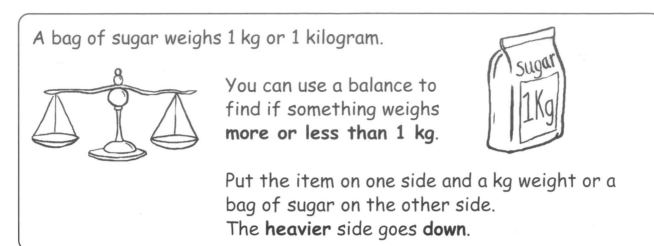

A bag of sugar weighs 1 kg or 1 kilogram.

You can use a balance to find if something weighs **more or less than 1 kg**.

Put the item on one side and a kg weight or a bag of sugar on the other side.
The **heavier** side goes **down**.

Choose 5 items. List them in the table under Item.

Tick a box to show if you think each item is less or more than 1 kg.

Check the weight with the balance. Tick the correct box.

Item	I think it weighs		Checked with the balance. It was	
	less than 1 kg	more than 1 kg	less than 1 kg	more than 1 kg

More or less than ½ kilogram

Divide a 1 kg bag of sugar into 2 equal bags.

Each bag = ½ kg (or 500 g)

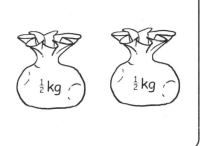

Choose 5 items. Write them in the table under Item.

Tick a box to show if you think each item is less or more than ½ kg.

Check the weight with the balance.
Tick the correct box.

Item	I think it weighs		Checked with the balance. It was	
	less than ½ kg	more than ½ kg	less than ½ kg	more than ½ kg

Choose a weight for each item:

a about 1 kg

b about ½ kg

c about 2 kg

d more than 3 kg

e about 1½ kg

You can:
- estimate the weight
- read the label.

2.2kg

1 kg
Mixed Fruit
ready washed

MILK
454 grams

Self raising flour
1.5 kg

Super Suds
3.3 kg

Every 10 kg are labelled.

The lines between show the kg.

There is 1 kg between each mark and the next.

You need the items listed in the table and other items.
Estimate the weight each item to the nearest kg.
Write your estimates in the table below.

Use scales to measure each weight. Put the results in the table.

Add more items to the list.

Item	Estimate (nearest kg)	Measured weight (nearest kg)
A bag		
A file		
A pile of 5 books		

Worksheets

Empty, full, more or less

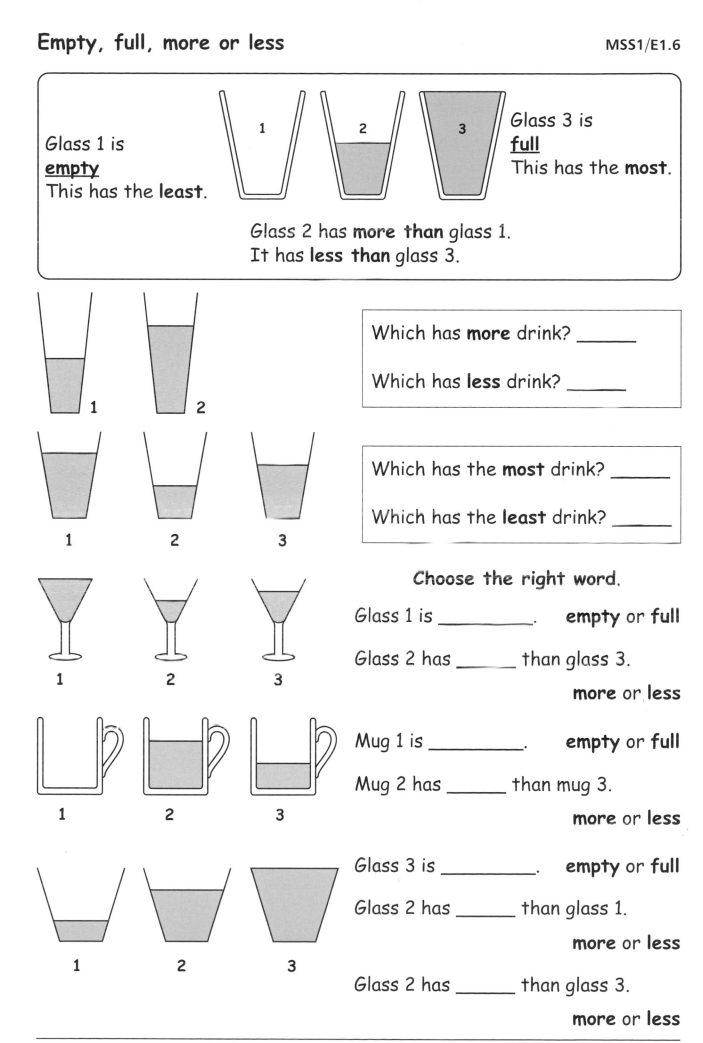

Glass 1 is
empty
This has the **least**.

Glass 3 is
full
This has the **most**.

Glass 2 has **more than** glass 1.
It has **less than** glass 3.

Which has **more** drink? _____

Which has **less** drink? _____

Which has the **most** drink? _____

Which has the **least** drink? _____

Choose the right word.

Glass 1 is _____.   **empty** or **full**

Glass 2 has _____ than glass 3.

more or less

Mug 1 is _____.   **empty** or **full**

Mug 2 has _____ than mug 3.

more or **less**

Glass 3 is _____.   **empty** or **full**

Glass 2 has _____ than glass 1.

more or **less**

Glass 2 has _____ than glass 3.

more or **less**

Worksheets

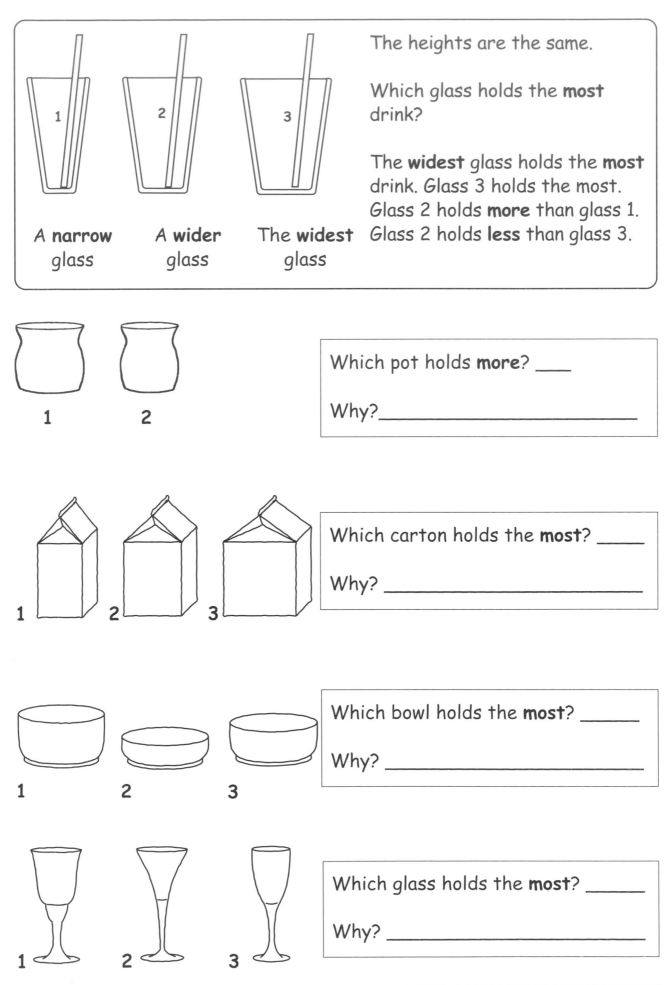

The heights are the same.

Which glass holds the **most** drink?

The **widest** glass holds the **most** drink. Glass 3 holds the most. Glass 2 holds **more** than glass 1. Glass 2 holds **less** than glass 3.

A **narrow** glass

A **wider** glass

The **widest** glass

Worksheets

1 2

Which pot holds **more**? ____

Why?_____

1 2 3

Which carton holds the **most**? _____

Why? _____

1 2 3

Which bowl holds the **most**? _____

Why? _____

1 2 3

Which glass holds the **most**? _____

Why? _____

Measure in cupfuls

You need:
- 5 different cups
- a kettle.

Label the cups.   **1   2   3   4   5**

Use cup 1.
Fill the kettle with cupfuls of water – count the cupfuls.
How many cupfuls are needed to fill the kettle?
Record the result in the table.

Cup	Number of cupfuls needed to fill the kettle
1	
2	
3	
4	
5	

Do the same with the other cups.

Do you think cups are an accurate way of
measuring how much a container holds? _____

Why? _____

_____

The amount a container will hold is called its **capacity**.

Understand capacity in litres and millilitres

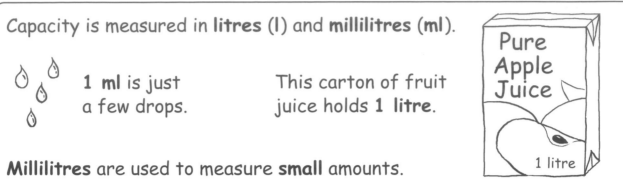

Capacity is measured in **litres** (l) and **millilitres** (ml).

1 ml is just a few drops.

This carton of fruit juice holds **1 litre**.

Pure Apple Juice

1 litre

Millilitres are used to measure **small** amounts.
Litres are used to measure **larger** amounts.

What would you use to measure the capacity of these items?
litres (l) or **millilitres** (ml)

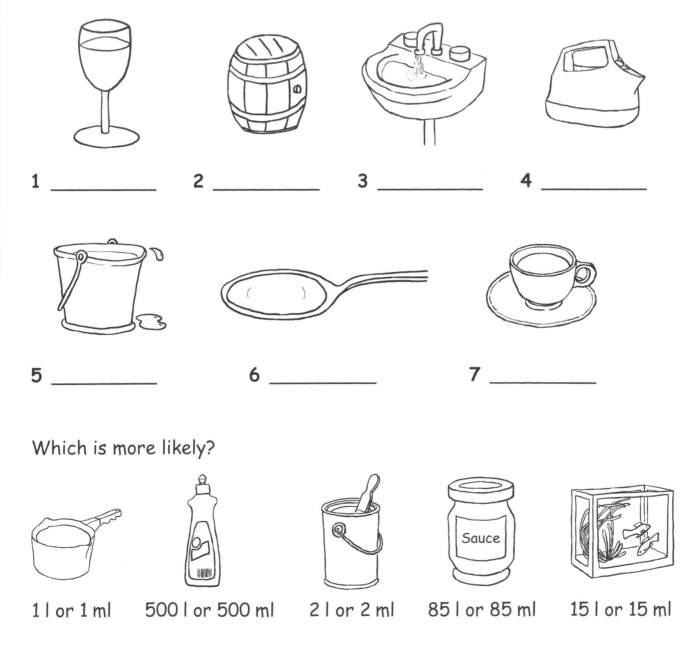

1 _____   2 _____   3 _____   4 _____

5 _____   6 _____   7 _____

Which is more likely?

1 l or 1 ml   500 l or 500 ml   2 l or 2 ml   85 l or 85 ml   15 l or 15 ml

Worksheets

More or less than a litre

You need a litre measuring jug.

Find the mark on the jug for 1 litre.

Choose 6 containers.
Label them 1, 2, 3, 4, 5 and 6.

Tick boxes in the table to show:

- which containers you think hold **less** than 1 litre

- which containers you think hold **more** than 1 litre.

To check:
Fill each container with water. Empty each into the measuring jug.
Is the water **over** the litre mark, or **under** the litre mark?
Tick the correct boxes.

Container	I think this holds		Check with the measuring jug	
	less than 1 litre	more than 1 litre	less than 1 litre	more than 1 litre
1				
2				
3				
4				
5				
6				

Worksheets

More or less than ½ litre

You need a measuring jug marked
with ½ litre or 500 ml.

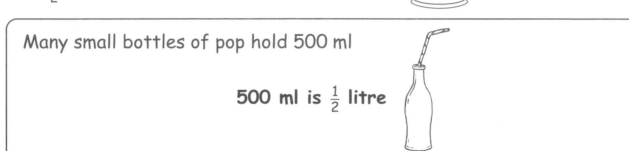

Many small bottles of pop hold 500 ml

500 ml is ½ litre

Fill a small pop bottle with water. Empty it into the measuring jug.

Does the pop bottle hold ½ litre (500 ml), more than 500 ml, or less than 500 ml?

Choose 5 containers.
Label them 1, 2, 3, 4 and 5.

Tick boxes in the table to show:

- which containers you think hold **less** than ½ litre
- which containers you think hold **more** than ½ litre.

To check:
Fill each container with water. Empty each into the measuring jug.
Is the water **over** the ½ litre (500 ml) mark, or **under** the ½ litre (500 ml) mark?
Tick the correct boxes.

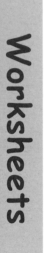

Worksheets

Container	I think this holds		Check with the measuring jug	
	less than ½ litre	more than ½ litre	less than ½ litre	more than ½ litre
1				
2				
3				
4				
5				

Maths the Basic Skills Curriculum Edition: Measures, Shape and Space Worksheet Pack © Nelson Thornes Ltd 2004

Estimate capacity

These both hold 1 litre.

How many litres do you think these hold?

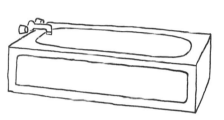

50 l, 250 l, or 500 l

2 l, 5 l, or 10 l

1 l, 10 l, or 20 l

20 l, 30 l, or 50 l

3 l, 30 l, or 100 l

10 l, 20 l or 30 l

1 l, 5 l, or 10 l

1 l, 5 l, or 10 l

10 l, 100 l, or 500 l

Worksheets

Hot or cold

Temperature is a measure of how hot or cold something is.
In the UK we measure temperature in **degrees Celsius** (°C).

30°C It's a very hot sunny day.
What would you wear?
(Draw arrows like this)

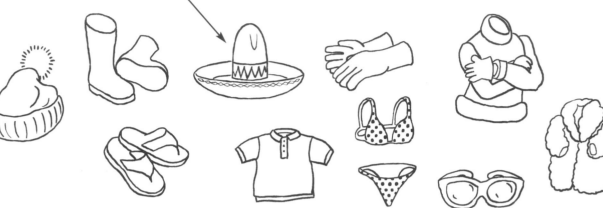

2°C It's cold.
What would you wear?

15°C It's warm.
What would you wear?

Draw arrows to show what you might do when the temperature is:

28°C   10°C   1°C?

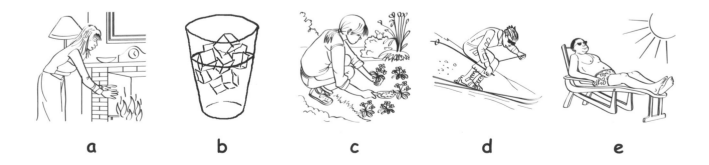

a   b   c   d   e

Warmer or cooler

Look at the temperatures on the map.

London is 23°C. Edinburgh is 16°C.

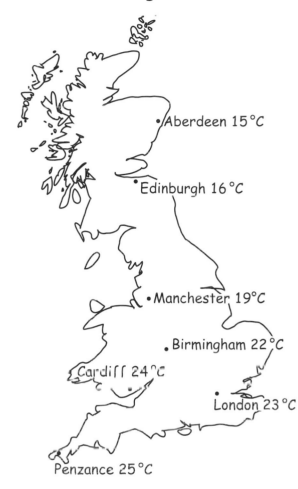

London is **warmer** than Edinburgh.

Edinburgh is **cooler** than London.

Add the word **warmer** or **cooler**.

Cardiff is _____ than London.

London is _____ than Cardiff.

Cardiff is _____ than Edinburgh

Edinburgh is _____ than Cardiff.

Penzance is _____ than London.

London is _____ than Penzance.

Manchester is _____ than Penzance.

Penzance is _____ than Manchester.

Aberdeen is _____ than Birmingham.

Birmingham is _____ than Aberdeen.

Worksheets

The temperatures are measured to the nearest degree.
Read the sentences below.
Fill in the missing temperatures on the map.

London is **colder** than Brussels, but **warmer** than Paris.

Bonn is **warmer** than Brussels, but **colder** than Amsterdam.

Berlin is **warmer** than Warsaw, but **colder** than Prague.

Dublin is **warmer** than Edinburgh, but **colder** than London.

Vienna is **colder** than Warsaw, but **warmer** than Bonn.

Berne is **colder** than Berlin, but **warmer** than Amsterdam.

Worksheets

Thermometers

Thermometers measure temperature.
Here is a thermometer.

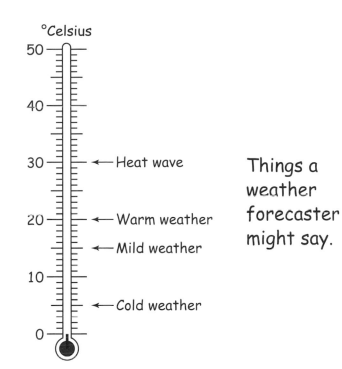

°Celsius

Things a
weather
forecaster
might say.

Write down the temperatures marked as:

a heat wave _____

warm weather _____

cold weather _____

Find the difference in the temperatures marked as:

a heat wave and mild weather _____

cold weather and warm weather _____

cold weather and a heat wave _____

Worksheets

Use a thermometer like this one.

Breathe on the thermometer several times.

What happens to the level of the liquid in the tube?

Put the thermometer in a bowl of **cold** water for 3 minutes.
What happens to the level of the liquid in the tube?

Put the thermometer in a bowl of **warm** water for 3 minutes.
What happens to the level of the liquid in the tube?

Put the thermometer in a bowl of **hot** water for 3 minutes.
What happens to the level of the liquid in the tube?

Put the thermometer outside for 3 minutes.
What happens to the level of the liquid in the tube?

Put the thermometer on the table for 3 minutes.
What happens to the level of the liquid in the tube?

Read a thermometer

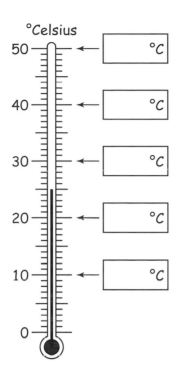

Write the temperatures marked by arrows in the boxes.

Draw arrows to show these temperatures on the thermometer.
Write the temperature beside each arrow.

5°C	15°C	25°C	35°C	45°C

The level of the liquid **rises** as the temperature gets **hotter**.
The level of the liquid **falls** as the temperature gets **colder**.
The liquid shows the temperature in ° Celsius.

What temperature is the liquid showing on the thermometer? _____

Colour the thermometer to show 32°C.

Read scales at home

What number setting is the fridge on?

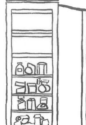

_____

These fridge dials are set between numbers.
Write down the **nearest** number setting on each.

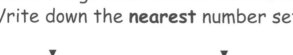

_____ _____ _____ _____

What settings are shown below?

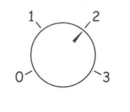
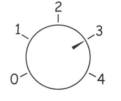
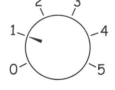

_____ _____ _____

Roughly what is the temperature set at?
Write down the **nearest** number.

_____ _____ _____

What temperature settings are shown below?

_____ _____ _____

Dials in the car

Ask yourself

What is the **nearest** number?
Is the pointer **before** that number?
Is the pointer **after** that number?

Approximately what is the speed of these cars?

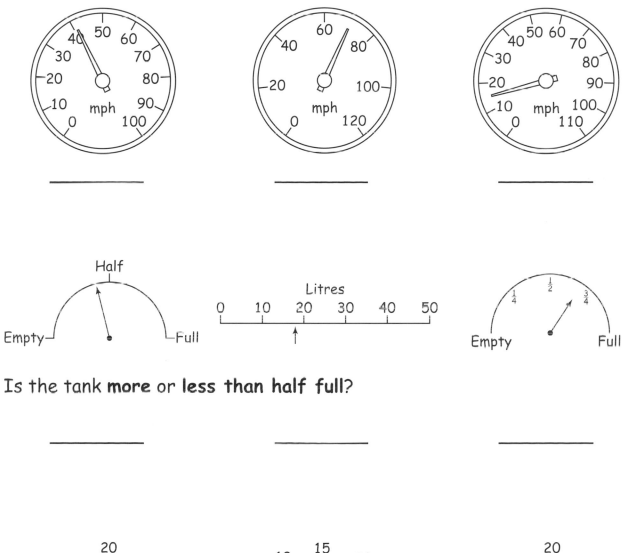

_____   _____   _____

Is the tank **more** or **less than half full**?

_____   _____   _____

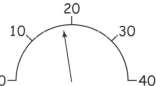 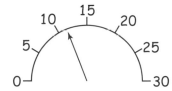 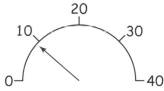

Approximately what is the temperature in the car?

_____   _____   _____

Worksheets

Look at this scale:

The 0, 10 and 20 are labelled.
There are 10 spaces (divisions) between the numbers.
Each division represents 1.

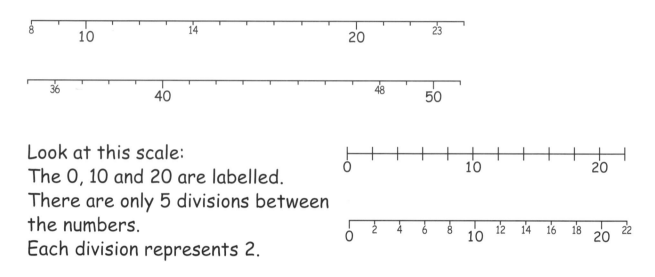

Fill in the missing numbers on these scales:

Look at this scale:
The 0, 10 and 20 are labelled.
There are only 5 divisions between
the numbers.
Each division represents 2.

Fill in the numbers at the markers on these scales:

What are the measurements shown by the arrows?

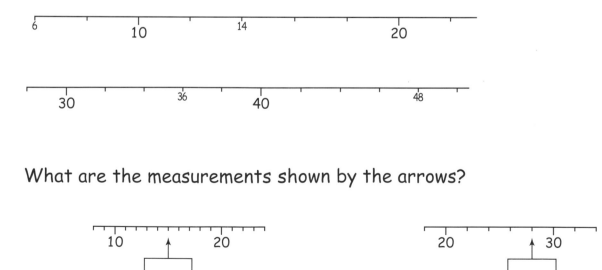

More gaps

Look at this scale:

```
|___|___|___|___|
0   10  20  30  40
```

0, 10, 20, 30 and 40 are labelled.
How many divisions are there
between 0 and 10? _____

Each division represents 5.

```
|   5   |   15  |   25  |   35  |
0       10      20      30      40
```

Fill in the missing numbers on these scales:

```
|  5  |     |     |     |     |     |     |  75 |
0     10    20    30    40          60
```

```
|     |     |     |     |     |  65 |     |     |  85 |
10    20    30          50
```

Look at this scale:
0, 20, 40, 60, 80, 100 are labelled.

```
|     |     |     |     |     |
0     20    40    60    80    100
```

Fill in the missing numbers – 10, 30, 50, 70 and 90.

Fill in the missing numbers on this scale.

```
|     |     |     |     |     |     |
0           20          40          60
```

What are the measurements shown by the arrows?

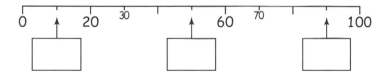

```
|     ↑   |  30 |     ↑  |  70 |     ↑  |
0        20          60          100
```

Worksheets

Squares

A square has:
- 4 sides – all the same length
- 4 square corners.

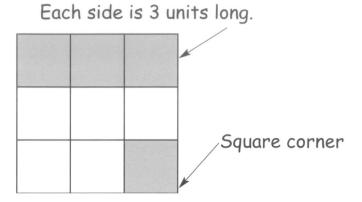

Each side is 3 units long.

Square corner

Tick the shapes that are square.

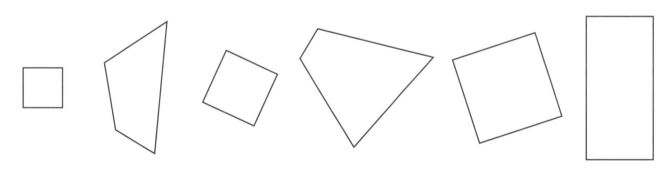

How many squares can you see in this pattern?

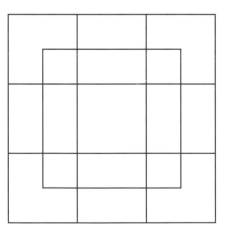

Complete these sentences:

A square has _____ sides and _____ corners.

All the sides are the _____ length.

Words to use:

four   same   square

Worksheets

Rectangles

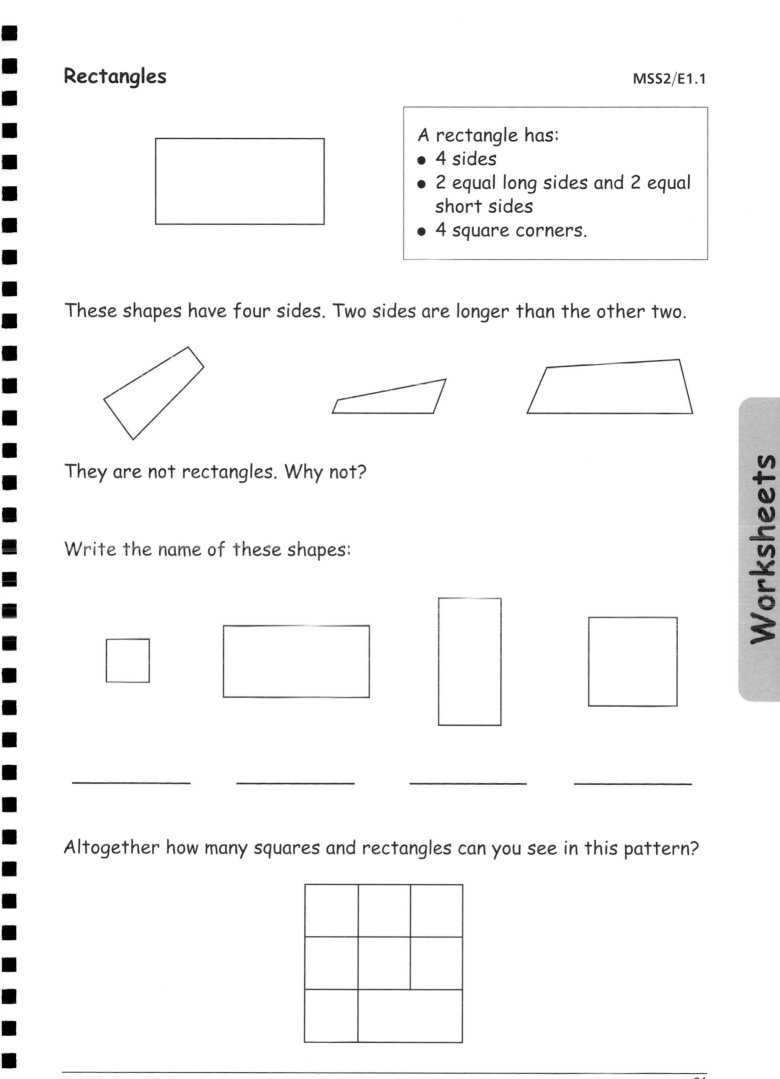

A rectangle has:
- 4 sides
- 2 equal long sides and 2 equal short sides
- 4 square corners.

These shapes have four sides. Two sides are longer than the other two.

They are not rectangles. Why not?

Write the name of these shapes:

_____   _____   _____   _____

Altogether how many squares and rectangles can you see in this pattern?

Worksheets

Circles

This is a **circle**.

Buttons and plates are in the shape of a circle.

 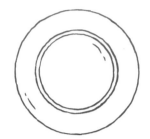

What other things are in the shape of a circle?

_____

How many circles can you see in this pattern?

Draw the missing circles to make the matching eyes.

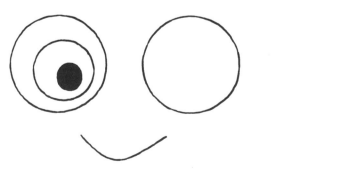 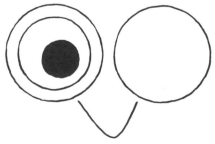

Worksheets

Which shape? – squares, circles and rectangles MSS2/E1.1

Draw the next shape in each pattern.

1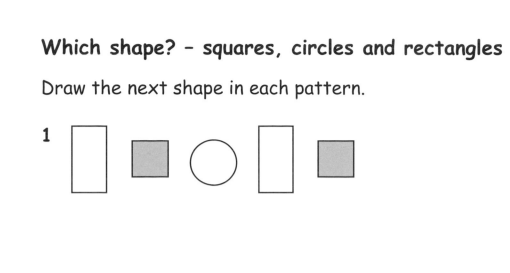

2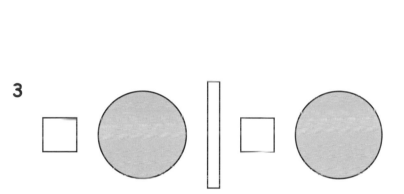

3

Write the name of each shape you have drawn.

Name the shapes of these signs:

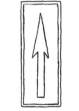

_____

_____

_____

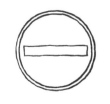

_____

_____

_____

Worksheets

Cubes and cuboids

A cube has:

- 6 **square faces**
- 12 **edges**
- 8 **corners**

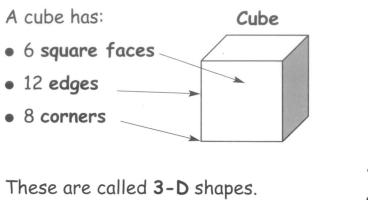

Cube

Cuboid

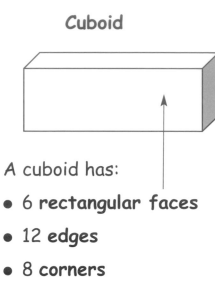

These are called **3-D** shapes.

A cuboid has:

- 6 **rectangular faces**
- 12 **edges**
- 8 **corners**

Write the name of its 3-D shape under each item.

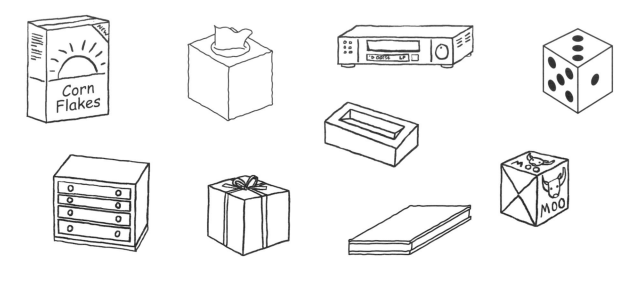

Look around you.
Write down 5 objects that are cuboids.

Can you see any cubes?

Complete these sentences:

A cube has 6 _____ faces.

A cuboid has 6 _____ faces.

Words to use:
square   **rectangular**

Worksheets

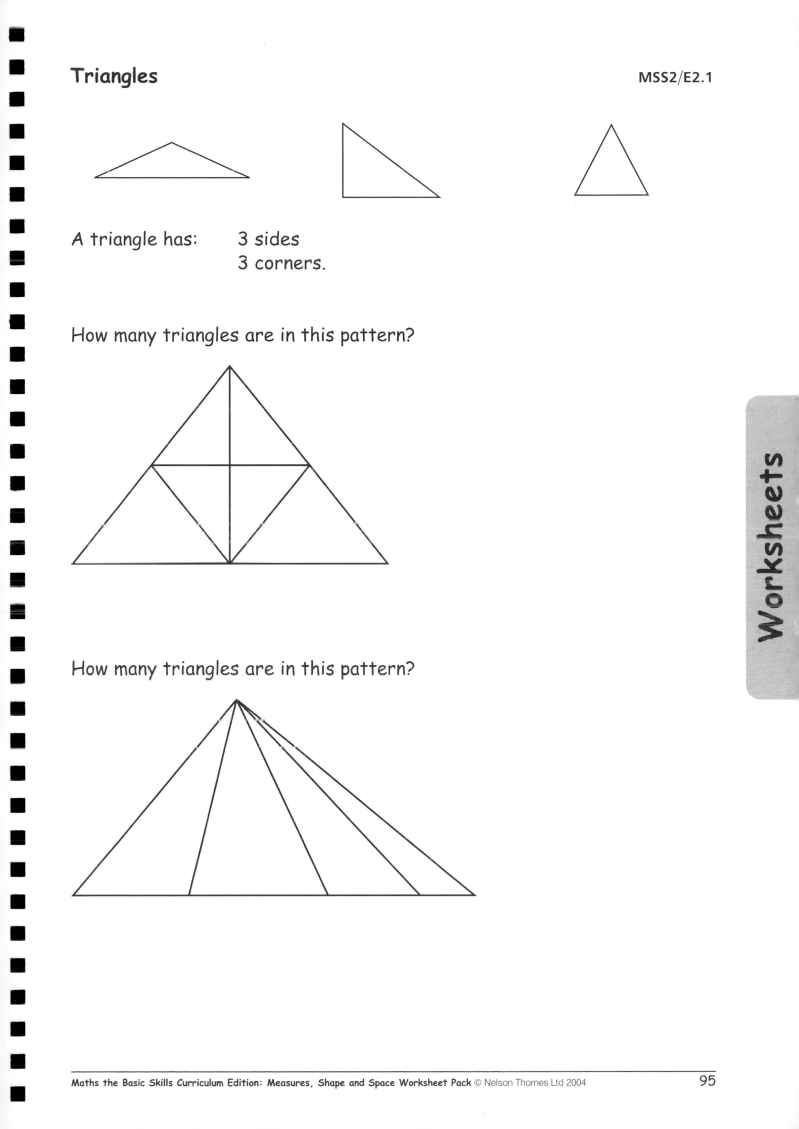

A triangle has: 3 sides
                   3 corners.

How many triangles are in this pattern?

How many triangles are in this pattern?

Shapes and signs

The shape of a road sign means something.

Circles – give **instructions**

Triangles – give **warnings**   **Rectangles** – give **information**

Are these signs giving an instruction, a warning, or information?

	Town centre 1 mile		

_____   _____   _____   _____

_____   _____   _____   _____

Here are some washing signs. The shape means something.
What does each shape give information about?

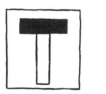

Can tumble dry   Do not tumble dry   Drip dry   Dry flat   _____

Can bleach   Do not bleach   _____

Pyramids and cylinders

The Egyptians built pyramids.

This pyramid has: a square base
4 triangular faces
8 edges
5 corners

It is a **square-based pyramid**.

This tin is a **cylinder**.

A cylinder has: • 2 circular faces
• a curved rectangular face
• 2 edges

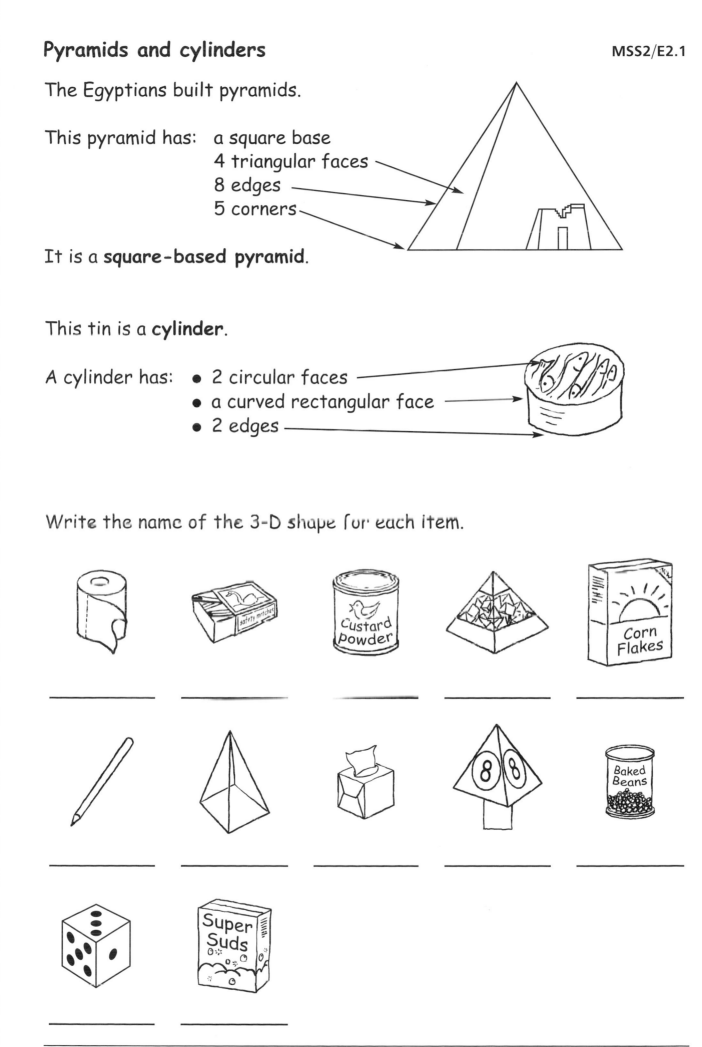

Write the name of the 3-D shape for each item.

_____ _____ _____ _____ _____

_____ _____ _____ _____ _____

_____ _____

Worksheets

Sides and corners (2-D shapes)

Complete the table.

	Number of sides	Number of corners
Square		
Rectangle		
Triangle		

Complete these sentences:

Words to use:		
short	same	long
square	corners	same

A rectangle usually has two _____ sides and two _____ sides.

The long sides are the _____ length and the short sides are the

_____ length. A rectangle has four _____

_____.

Which shape has three sides and three corners?   _____

A square and a rectangle are alike in many ways.

Is a square always a rectangle? _____

Is a rectangle always a square? _____

Worksheets

2-D faces on 3-D shapes

Write the shape of the **faces** on each 3-D shape.

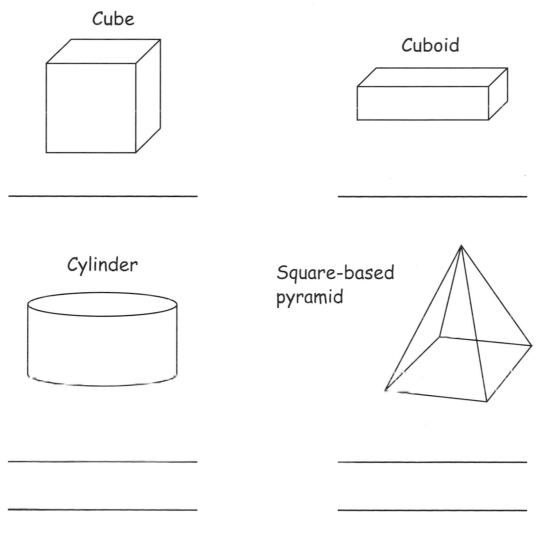

Cube

Cuboid

_____

_____

Cylinder

Square-based
pyramid

_____

_____

_____

_____

Which shapes have only flat faces?

Which shape has flat and curved faces?

Name these 3-D shapes.

Worksheets

Make a cube and cuboid

Cut out these shapes. Fold along the dotted lines.
Join the **edges** together, using the tabs.

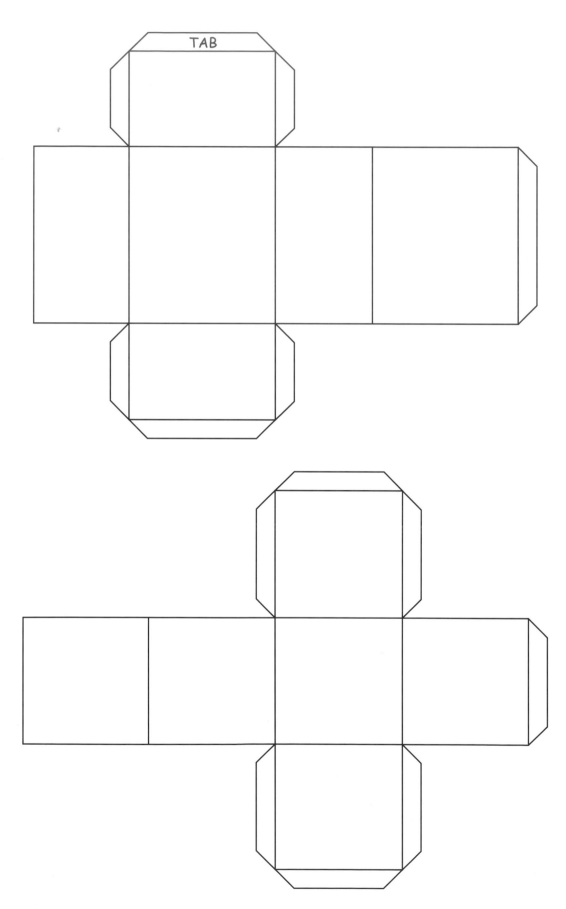

TAB

Maths the Basic Skills Curriculum Edition: Measures, Shape and Space Worksheet Pack © Nelson Thornes Ltd 2004

Worksheets

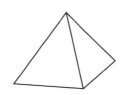

Find some cuboids, cubes, cylinders and square-based pyramids.

For each shape count the:
- number of faces
- number of edges
- number of corners

Complete the table.

	Number of sides	Number of corners
Cube		
Cuboid		
Cylinder		
Square-based pyramid		

What is the difference between a cube and a cuboid? _____

_____

A cuboid can have 3 measurements for length, width and height.

A cube only needs 1 measurement. Why? _____

_____

Complete these sentences:

Words to use:
circular   two   rectangular   square
triangular   five   eight

A cylinder has two _____
faces and one curved _____ face.
It has _____ edges.

A square-based pyramid has one _____ face and four _____ faces.
It has _____ edges and _____ corners.

Worksheets

Between, inside, near

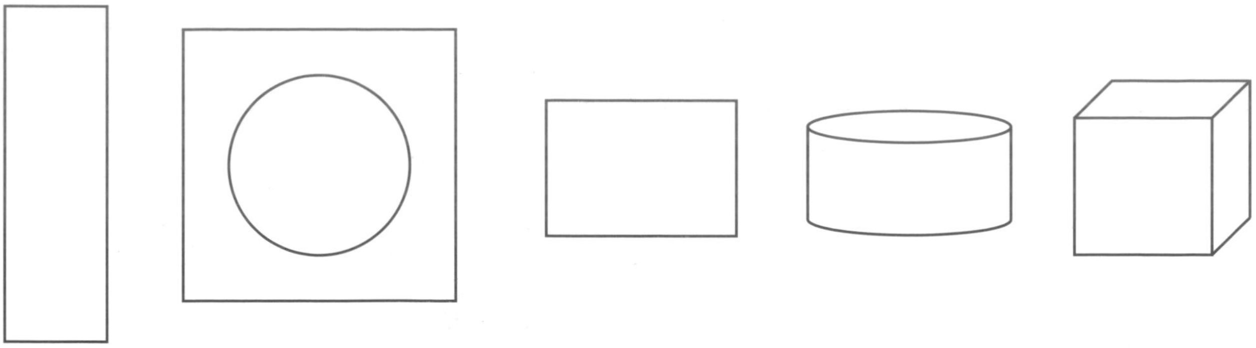

The square is **between** the rectangles.
The circle is **inside** the square.
The cube is **near** the cuboid.

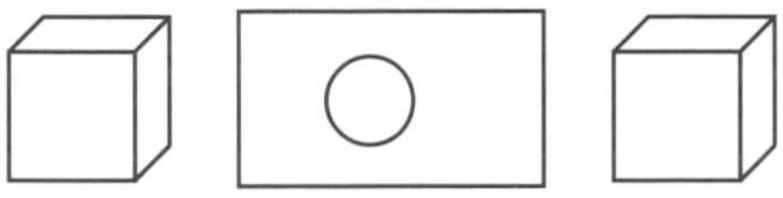

Where is the circle? _____ the rectangle

Where is the rectangle? _____ the cubes

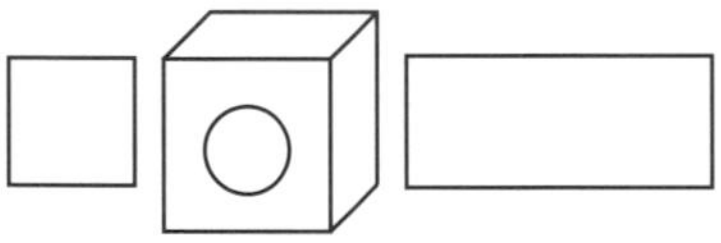

Where is the circle? _____ the cube

_____ the square

_____ the square and the rectangle

Draw a square **between** the rectangles.
Draw a circle **inside** the square.

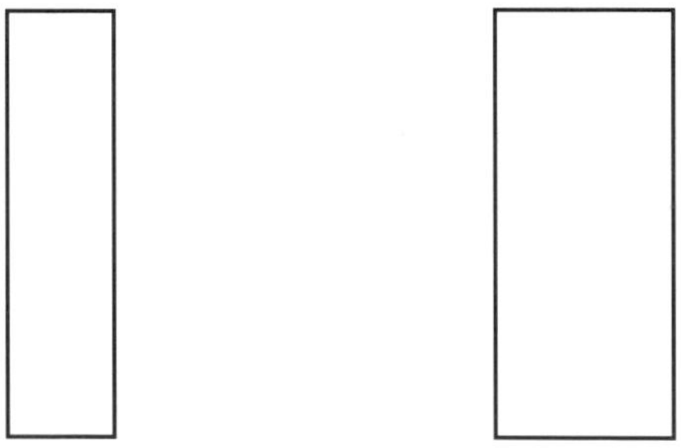

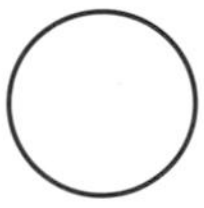

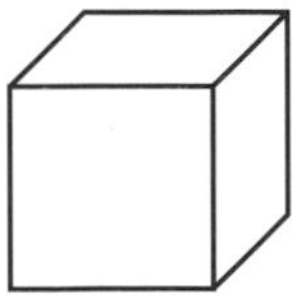

Draw a rectangle **near** the circle.
Draw a square **near** the cube.

Worksheets

The crisps are **to the left** of the videos.
The nuts are **to the right** of the videos.
The chocolate box is **above** the videos.
The biscuits and pens are **below** the videos.
The biscuits are **behind** the pens.
The pens are **in front** of the biscuits.

What is to the **right** of the videos? _____

What is to the **left** of the nuts? _____

What is **above** the biscuits? _____

What is **below** the chocolate box? _____

What is **behind** the matches? _____

What is in **front** of the cans of cola? _____

These shelves need filling.

Write rice **to the left** of the peanuts.

Write beans **to the right** of the peanuts.

Write books **above** the peanuts.

Write eggs **below** the peanuts.

Draw a bag of sugar **behind** the peanuts.

Draw a circle **in front** of the peanuts.

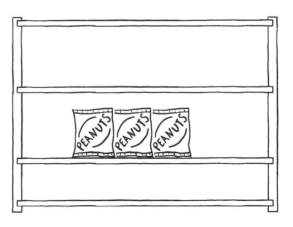

Tell the time

What is the time on these clocks?

Maths the Basic Skills Curriculum Edition: Measures, Shape and Space Worksheet Pack © Nelson Thornes Ltd 2004

Monday	Tuesday
Wednesday	Thursday
Friday	Saturday
Sunday	

Seasons of the year

Winter	Spring
Summer	Autumn

Resources

What happens in the different seasons of the year?

Spring	Summer
It starts to get warmer.	It should be hot.
Autumn	**Winter**
The days get shorter.	It's cold.

Resources

People play in the snow.	Birds build nests.	The leaves need raking.
People sunbathe.	There is snow on the hills.	People start planting seeds.
Shops get ready for Christmas.	The leaves are falling.	Lots of people go on holiday.
It's bonfire night.	Flowers start to grow.	It's sunny.
We wear lots of clothes to keep warm.	People start working in the garden.	Nuts fall off the trees.

Resources

January	February	March
April	May	June
July	August	September
October	November	December
Jan	Feb	Mar
Apr	May	Jun
Jul	Aug	Sep
Oct	Nov	Dec

Maths the Basic Skills Curriculum Edition: Measures, Shape and Space Worksheet Pack © Nelson Thornes Ltd 2004

Resources

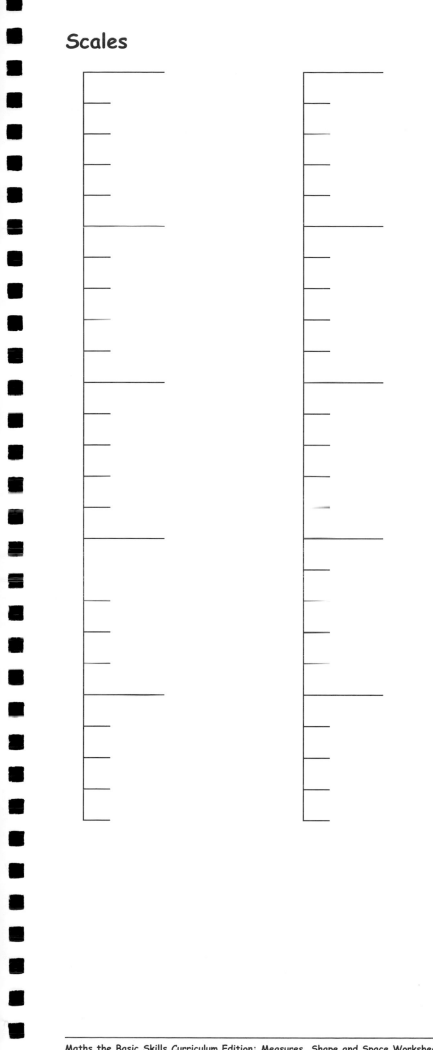

Resources

Maths the Basic Skills Curriculum Edition: Measures, Shape and Space Worksheet Pack © Nelson Thornes Ltd 2004

Resources

Resources